O/S 003915   5⁰⁰

D0977586

Being

OTHER BOOKS BY LEE COIT

Listening:
How to Increase Awareness of Your Inner Guide

Accepting:
How to Increase Your Awareness of Perfection

Please visit the Hay House Website at:
http://www.hayhouse.com

Being

How to Increase Your Awareness of Oneness

LEE COIT

Hay House, Inc.
Carlsbad, CA

Copyright © 1997 by Lee Coit

Published and distributed in the United States by:
Hay House, Inc., P.O. Box 5100, Carlsbad, CA 92018-5100
(800) 654-5126 • (800) 650-5115 (fax)

Edited by: Jill Kramer   *Designed by:* Jenny Richards

All rights reserved. No part of this book may be reproduced by any
mechanical, photographic, or electronic process, or in the form of a
phonographic recording, nor may it be stored in a retrieval system, trans-
mitted, or otherwise be copied for public or private use—other than for
"fair use" as brief quotations embodied in articles and reviews without
prior written permission of the publisher.

Library of Congress Cataloging-in-Publication Data

Coit, Lee.
    Being :   how to increase your awareness of oneness   /   Lee Coit.
        p.   cm.
    ISBN   1-56170-405-9
    1. Spiritual life.   2. Self-perception—Religious aspects.
I. Title.
BL624.C632   1997   96-36546
291.4'2—dc20   CIP

                        ISBN 1-56170-405-9

                    00 99 98 97   4 3 2 1
                    First Printing, May 1997

            Printed in the United States of America

Contents

Foreword

As Lee's ex-wife, I hold the unique position of reading about myself in this book, and the spiritual crisis I had a part in precipitating for Lee when I left our marriage. The very fact that Lee asked me to write the Foreword to this book demonstrates how deeply he has moved into a state of BEING, which is where betrayal isn't possible and only love exists. Especially courageous on his part is the fact that he didn't ask to read this before it went to his publisher. Now you may think that's because we have remained close friends since the divorce. We have not, but I realize now as I read this book that the reason for that has been my own guilt over leaving a perfectly wonderful man, especially when God brought us together!

As Lee describes in this book, we believe early on in the listening process that listening will help us reach our goals easier. And it does. What I believed, though, was that if you reached a fantasy through guidance, that it would make you happy. I learned, however, that God totally supports us in fulfilling our fantasies, because that's the shortest path to the realization that no fantasy gives you what you are searching for—that the only fulfillment comes from completely accepting your own Divine essence, and that of everyone else's.

One of my fantasies was to find a "spiritual" man who shared my vision and who was doing similar work to myself so that we could share everything. I found that with Lee when I moved to the retreat with him, and we traveled all over the world leading workshops together. Imagine my shock when three years after our marriage, I found myself sliding into a severe depression. It didn't seem possible to me, as I had everything in my life I had ever wanted, and it had all been brought to me through guidance!

I prayed and struggled with my despair, asking for direction about what to do. It did not seem to come. I realize now that I was getting plenty of help, but I was not willing to hear it, as it did not match my concept of God and guidance. God couldn't possibly lead me to something and then lead me away from it, could he? My whole being was screaming to leave the retreat, come down off the mountaintop, and get on with my life. I tried to talk Lee into selling the retreat, and he agreed. But he wasn't truly ready to let it go, as his story in this book reveals.

Finally, I simply left, with no notice and little explanation. I could not explain my actions at that time because I didn't remotely understand why I was leaving. I only knew that I had to or I would drown. I felt so guilty. Most of my friends and family members judged and rejected me.

I have since realized that everything about that decision was guided. I was led on to the experiences in my life that have been necessary for my own path in awareness. One of the biggest lessons for me was a key point in this book. And that is total acceptance of one's own essence. Just as I blamed Lee for persisting beyond all reason with the retreat, he blamed me for leaving him for no reason. The truth is that sooner or later our paths would have diverged anyway due to the core differences in our essence. My essence is change. A big part of his is persistence. Until this experience, I never valued my essence. In fact, I was always trying to make myself more stable, consistent, and persistent. I found I could only do that for so long before something in me would snap, and off I would go into the next dramatic life change. I now accept that since change is a big part of me, it will cause me to upset a lot of people around me who want me to stay the same. It causes me to be in the unpopular position of catalyst at times, which I have hated, because all I ever wanted was to be loved.

I am so grateful that Lee has written this book. In it are profound truths expressed in an accessible way. Lee's search for meaning, and his struggles along the way, have made him a great teacher—based on personal experience, not theory.

Lee has written me wonderful letters, thanking me for the part I played in his own "dark night of the soul." I couldn't believe they were real. I now see that it was my own guilt about following my own path and for hurting him. I now understand that I needed to leave him in order to trust my own inner guide completely again. I had begun to surrender what felt right for me, to try and learn, just as he has, that my inner connection to Source is all that I can count on to never change. That the form of everything else can and will keep failing to meet my expectations, and that as long as I stay open and willing to accept what is happening, and most importantly to accept myself and others, that all will be well.

Just relax, be fully yourself, and know that you are loved BECAUSE of your flaws as much as for your strengths. You are God's perfect creation now—not at some future point in time. And so is everyone else!

Thank you, Lee, for being fully yourself, and for sharing your heart and process with the rest of us.

— Vikki Hansen

Introduction

Twenty years ago, I decided to devote all my efforts to finding the secrets of a happy and peaceful life. At the time, my life was anything but that. However, my search has been more successful than I ever expected. It has uncovered a direct connection with a Divine Source that provides me with more than I need. This Source, which I call God, has shown me how to live in a world filled with limitations in an unlimited way. My first book, *Listening,* details how I connect with this source. My second book, *Accepting,* explains how to use this connection in everyday life and find peace. As I finished writing the second book, my Source gave me the final step in this three-step process. It is called *Being,* and can best be described as noninterference with Reality. *Being* reveals my true identity and oneness with all Creation.

Each book is the culmination of years of proving that these methods work by living them. I really never set out to write any of these books; they just seem to emerge on their own. My intention has always been to discover these secrets for my personal use. I pass these processes along to you, knowing that they provide all the tools you need to live a joy-filled existence here and now. Here's how *Listening, Accepting,* and *Being* came about and how they work together to give me an unlimited existence.

Before I discovered *listening* and began using it in my personal life, I had used a form of it in my advertising agency business for nearly 15 years. I did not think of it as spiritual; it was just a technique I used to come up with creative ideas. When I was given a problem, I would gather all the information about it and then just be quiet and wait. Eventually, wonderful solutions would come to me. Sometimes it happened right away, and sometimes days later at the very last minute. I did not think of answers; in fact, it helped not to think about the problem but just to let the ideas emerge in their own time. Many ideas came to me during this waiting period, but when the right one arrived, I always got an immediate flash of clarity and recognition.

After I left the advertising business, I was seeking answers for my personal problems. It was then that I discovered a more expanded version of this creative ability that I called *listening*. This was a truly unique source of information unlike anything I had experienced before. I could ask about anything and get wonderful answers from this superior source. Eventually, a dialogue with this inner voice became possible. Nearly a year went by before I realized that *listening* was very similar to what I had been doing in the advertising business. In the beginning, these two processes felt very different despite the fact that they both came from my being quiet and waiting. When I was intuitive in the advertising business, the ideas seemed to come from my own talent. When I first became aware of *listening*, it felt as if the answers came from a superior intelligence beyond my own.

Accepting, the next step, developed as an outgrowth of the *listening* process. The more I *listened* for solutions to my problems, the more I realized that I was being given the ability to see things in a new way. When I saw things around me clearly, I seldom needed to change anything. In short, I did not have to use my judgment or *listen* to decide what to do. I could just *accept* everything that happened to me and then *listen* to find out why it was in my life. Instead of avoiding certain people and situations, now I could embrace everything. *Accepting* is a form of forgiveness that frees me and the world from the distortion of my judgment. This second step was revolutionary in changing my view of the world, because now I did not have to control it.

Being, the third step, changes my relationship with everything, including myself. It shows me that everything is connected to and part of me. It is not part of the crazy me I often identify with, but is part of my natural self. *Being* asks me to release my concepts of who I am and allow my spiritual identity to emerge. If I do, all my activity is in easy harmony with what is occurring. There is no need, no strain, and no stress. *Being* places me beyond the world's effects and allows me to live at a different level of consciousness. Interestingly enough, the one question I have been told over and over to ask is, "What do I really want?" The answer to this question begins to reveal my *being*.

I have described these three processes separately, but

they are really one process. They are not progressive except that the development of a good *listening* attitude is essential before one can proceed further. As I have loosened my grip on the belief that I needed to figure out and control events, my life has become richer.

This book will help you release your limiting concepts so that your spiritual reality can emerge. Currently, there is great confusion in the self-help field about what is spiritual and what is material. Most self-improvement books tell you how to make the human being more spiritual. My path is very different, as you will see. A very good human being is still a human being. The two levels of consciousness can never mix. Becoming a good human being is a worthy goal and better in most cases than staying a very limited human being, but both are a far cry from an unlimited spiritual *being*. Throughout my entire life, I have been exposed to various self-improvement methods from positive thinking to mind control. I have utilized many of them in my life, and the results were the creation of a fairly successful human being. This success, however, never brought me the peace and happiness I was seeking. No matter what I accomplished, there was always some new goal to attain and something that needed to be changed.

In the late 1970s, I stopped all my efforts to find happiness using these methods and decided to find what was missing in my search. The last 20 years has seen a great expansion of my awareness and the discovery of the secret to inner peace and happiness. I now know that our current level of consciousness, which we call reality, is merely an illusion. There is another level of consciousness beyond our current one that is easily attainable and which *is* Reality. We find ourselves at present in the consciousness of an illusion that is similar to, but very different from, Reality. Writing about these two different consciousnesses can be confusing since the same words have different meanings when used to describe each level of awareness. So when I refer to these terms in a spiritual context such as Reality, Truth, and Love, I will capitalize them for clarity. When these terms are used to represent concepts on the human level, they will start with lower-case letters. The italicized words are terms I use that have special meaning to me, as described in my writings.

I hope to encourage you to seek the spiritual Life for its own sake and not as a means of promoting your human success. If, first and foremost, you seek the path that leads to Reality, then your human manifestation will take the form that most assists your quest. Give no thought to this form and the concepts attached to it, and it will never limit you. If you give any attention to human concepts, you provide them with all the power they have. This is the key to your spiritual growth.

In the beginning, I thought, as do many people, that *listening* to a Divine Source was a better way to get what I wanted. Ah! At that time, my spiritual life seemed simple. However, as my spiritual path has unfolded, the challenge to my personal core beliefs has been intense. This book covers the most painful yet expansive period in my human life to date. During these years, my human being has greatly diminished, while my spiritual *being* has become my true identity.

CHAPTER I

We Are Spiritual *Beings*

My Balloon Bursts

In the late 1980s, my pat spiritual answers to life's problems began to fail. My frustration grew as things refused to work out, despite the efforts I made to *listen*. For more than ten years, *listening* had brought me all I could hope for and much more. Now it seemed that nothing I did worked. This frustration was centered around my most cherished accomplishments at the time, such as building a retreat center, publishing my books, and having a loving relationship. All of these events had come into my life through inner guidance and seemed to hold the promise of a beautiful future. During the next five years, numerous things occurred that were difficult both personally and financially, and they will be used as examples throughout this book.

In the early 1990s, the *accepting* process had just been given to me, and I had just finished publishing the material. I was putting it into practice by not protecting myself, not avoiding situations that were unpleasant, and most of all, by suspending my judgment, which I was finding greatly flawed. Giving up my judgment was most challenging because I had always prided myself on having keen insight. In short, I was learning that I not only *should not* judge, but that I *could not* judge.

Over and over, my appraisal of situations was turning out wrong. I was told by my inner guide not to judge anything but to *accept* everything. As I stopped trying to figure things out, a second challenge arose. I was compelled to change my view of who I was. I was asked to give up the belief that I was a vulnerable creature living in a world that could harm me. In the beginning, as I tried not to defend myself, I felt more attacked than ever before. In time I realized that these attacks were not directed at me but at the concepts I held about myself. That was a very big difference, and the awareness was very freeing. Through using the process of *accepting,* I was shown that every concept I created about myself eventually became a limitation. Every upset I felt about attacks on my concepts was helpful, for it pointed out these self-imposed limitations.

Finding My Way

Where had my spiritual path gone? I think that was the most difficult question I faced during this period. In 1982, with a small devoted group of spiritual seekers, I helped start the Las Brisas Retreat Center. It was a beautiful place for people to come and find their spiritual connection and was located in the mountains of Southern California. While it was just an hour or so from Los Angeles and San Diego, it was a world apart. The center was located near a national forest so it was very quiet and serene. However, it could only be reached by going over miles of bad roads, and it was a fairly primitive facility in that it did not have normal phone service and generated its own power mostly from the sun.

At first, my path seemed clear, especially when the group disbanded after a few years and I took on the whole responsibility for the center. I was eager to create and nurture this wonderful haven and to preserve the natural environment. As the years passed, problems arose with land developers, and the cost of maintaining the center skyrocketed. After a time, I struggled with the burden of ownership. Then I felt that I was supposed to move on, especially after my marriage ended. Finally, it took a great deal of energy and money to sustain the facility and a lot of pain and frustration to complete the leaving process. For a while, I consoled myself with the idea that I would move when the right people come to take over the retreat center, but I hated *being* in a waiting mode. I longed to get on with my life and felt that my job as caretaker was too restrictive. In all honesty, I was not a happy *being*. What changed my frustration to joy and opened my eyes to my new path was that *I gave up!* Let me share how this happened, because giving up is often the hardest thing to do.

During my last four years at the retreat center, I sold it three times and then got it back each time after less than a year. Each time I got it back, a great deal of time and money were required to return it to the condition necessary to make it financially viable. The last time I had to repossess it, it was in such bad shape that I didn't know what to do. The previous owner had even left the taxes and assessments unpaid, and now they were going to have penalties attached. I had run out of both the energy and the resources to carry on. I had asked God many times what to do about the retreat with little success, but now I was really desperate. I had no more money, the situation seemed impossible, and I was not getting any clear direction.

One morning after another meditation, which again gave me no clear answers, I was totally out of patience. I was sitting on my bed too drained to start another day, and I cried out loud, "What do I have to do to get out of here?" The answer came quickly. It was: "Just leave." I had to smile. I had tried in vain to get clarity for years. I had slowly given up all my ideas about what the retreat should be, who should buy it, and what was a fair price. I had even given up hoping to get any of my investment back. I had explored various methods of selling the property and thought I was about as willing to let anything happen as I could be. Yet this was the first time I was willing to just pack up and let it all go. It seemed like a wonderful solution, and certainly it was not one I had ever considered since I had a firm grip on the concept that I always had to be successful. Leaving all the problems and just walking away represented failure to me. Now, however, I was at last ready to fail.

The only reason I did not leave that morning was that I owed a friend some $30,000 dollars on a second mortgage, and I knew that if I left, she might never get paid. I knew the equity in the retreat would easily pay off the main mortgage holders and the tax obligations, but her position was not as secure. I was determined to leave as soon as she could be reimbursed regardless of any other considerations. With this final giving up, the whole picture changed. I had been dealing with potential buyers who had made various wild proposals to me, none of which seemed valid. They had dragged their escrow on for more than six months so I demanded that they at least pay $30,000 up front so I could pay my friend as part of the sale. Despite their promises and reassurance that it was no problem, they never came up with the money, and their escrow expired. Of course, they had a new proposal and continued to try to buy the property, but then something wonderful happened.

Within three days, a totally new buyer with the money to make the project a success came forth, and I was able to not only pay all my debts, but to have enough left over to purchase a small house. The home I eventually bought was one I had seen in a vision several years before when I had asked where I would live next. I had seen a view of the ocean at the end of a small green valley. I had run across a house with this view nearly a year before, and thinking the retreat was sold at that time, I had made an offer to buy it. It was a perfect house for me, and I was very excited at the time. However, as a result of the delay in the retreat sale, my escrow failed and the house in my vision was sold to someone else.

At the time, it was just another failure in a long list of failures. I remember thinking when this happened that even my visions weren't working anymore. I had found my last three houses as the result of visions, but now that was gone, also. Imagine my surprise when I found out that not only was the house back on the market, but it had been fixed up and was being offered at less than the original price. My new buyer completed the Retreat sale in less than 30 days, and I was able to move into my dream house in just a few weeks. My vision had not failed after all; just my timing was off.

Incidentally, the new owner of the Las Brisas Conference Center is doing fine. He has purchased the additional acreage that was part of the original retreat vision and plans to expand the facility so larger groups of people can stay there. He and his family are delighted with their new home, and they hope to maintain and nurture this beautiful environment for many years. His plans for Las

Brisas are very compatible with those of the original founders, who include myself. I am so glad that it turned out as it did even though I was ready to accept any solution at the time.

Letting go is simple if we recognize the concepts we are holding on to. It is often hard to recognize them because they are usually such a basic part of our thinking. In this case, my concept was that success is always part of God's plan. That made it impossible for me to ever consider the option of failing. I had always believed that if I worked hard enough, I could eventually solve any problem. That concept had been useful most of my life, but now I had to let it go since I had outgrown it. Success and failure are not relevant to God but only to the human mind. This was my first real willingness to fail, and I count it now as my greatest success. Failure is still a tough choice, but it is now a new option for me. I am taken care of regardless of injustice, failure, unfairness, or any human concepts. I can trust God's direction and not let my point of view limit my actions. If God wants me to fail in terms of the world's view, I must be willing to do so. After all, it is only an illusion.

The Need to Judge Dies

The final outcome of this difficult period has been that I now know that each event has the potential to become a blessing. I know that I am the creator of my experiences and the decider of their outcomes. I do not need to judge others, for they have nothing to do with what is happening. Nor can God be blamed for my problems. Maybe like me, you have experienced that your good works do not protect you in times of need, nor do they always bring you love and approval. Instead of getting love, our kindness is often used against us. At first, this was very discouraging, but no more. The recognition of what is really happening has been a major breakthrough in finding my peace and joy. The problem is not with God or His Laws. They work perfectly all the time. In God's Creation, the Real World, everything operates flawlessly. We can, however, choose not to be conscious of Reality. In Chapter 4, we will discuss how our belief in dualism, a power apart from God, creates a false reality and traps us in a conflict that is not real. As we give up our judgment, which operates only in this reality, we begin to clearly see the illusory nature of this experience. The judgment of illusory things is without meaning and has no effect.

Learning We Are Lovable

When I was in the advertising business, I worked with many talented and physically beautiful people. They appeared to have it made, and I often wished I could be as attractive and self-confident as they seemed to be. As I got to know these people, I found to my surprise that they carried the same self-doubts and lack of esteem that I did. I am convinced that no one walks the earth who is free of self-doubt regarding their perceived shortcomings.

How can we ever get to the point where we can love ourselves? As long as we think we are human, I don't think we can. No self-improvement program can fix us up enough to overcome our self-doubts. The wonderful answer to the question, "What can I do to really improve myself?" is "Nothing." Be still and you will hear the real answer: "You are all perfect, now." We are not going to be, working to be, or learning to be, perfect. Our efforts to improve the human concept of who we are does nothing to change the Reality that we are spiritual *beings*. We were created perfect by God, and the only problem is that we are not aware of who we really are. The perfect us is the only us, and this cannot be changed. Our worth is not determined by our beauty, our mind, or our accomplishments. The only change we need is to expand our awareness.

This perfection is easy to see if you try. It is not temporary or illusory. You see this perfection in others nearly every day. People see this perfection in you nearly every day. When? When we share love. Think of those whom you love a great deal. Is your love based on how they look or how smart they are? Isn't it something deeper, something that is indescribable? They may not be perfect in terms of the world's definition, but they are perfect in your eyes as a parent, friend, or lover. Your awareness of their perfection is a decision you made when you decided to love them. Seeing perfection is a choice, a choice to love.

We can make this decision about everyone regardless of how they look or act, or whether they do what we want. We can start with a decision to unconditionally love one person. You have probably done that several times. Now we can keep extending this decision to more and more of God's Creation. Gratitude and *acceptance* are ways of constantly deciding to let God's Creation reveal itself. If we choose to see more people each day as perfect, then we will experience the blessing of Love in our life. Now we are seeing the Truth that is always there, and our only job is to continue to look for it everywhere. This is a natural and easy path that requires little except your desire for inner peace.

Believing we live in a conflicted world, we make plans to draw some people to us and to avoid others. When our plans do not work, we become stressed, believing that our human desires are the keys to our happiness. The harder we try to get what we think we need, the more frustrated we become. The more we fail to control, the more we seek to control. So the cycle continues. The answer to ending this cycle is to be still and know God's Creation is here and now. All we need is to choose to experience perfection. We demonstrate this choice by not judging. We make this decision by letting go of our desires and plans for others and our self.

In my experience, this letting go is not a sacrifice of what I want. It is getting to the point where I don't want whatever it is anymore. For example, the main thing I have been seeking all my life is a perfect loving relationship. My lack of success has made me realize that I cannot find love by using my own seeking processes. Instead of finding the right person to love, I am told to love everyone who comes into my life. Most of all, I am to love myself. Now what is happening is very exciting. I am finding love all around me. It's fine for me to want love in my life, but I need to give up the idea that I know how it will appear. Through a desire to see everything as lovable, I connect with the Divine Source and receive all the Love I need in the form I need when I need it.

Let's see how *being* naturally brings joy and happiness into our lives.

*Giving
unconditional love
to everyone includes
giving
unconditional love to
yourself.*

CHAPTER 2

The Natural State of *Being*

Being *Is Oneness*

*B*eing is the realization of our oneness with the Divine Source and all creation. Oneness is a natural state that exists with or without our awareness. In our present limited manifestation, few of us spend much time in this consciousness. However, we all have moments when we experience an awareness that is beyond our usual range. This expanded consciousness is experienced, for example, when we feel deep love for another, when we have a creative or an intuitive awareness, and when we are in awe of creation's beauty and grandeur. In these instances, we glimpse the potential of Reality. This happens to everyone at some time, but it is usually momentary and fleeting. This is our natural state. We cannot attain a state of *being* through mental effort or by using our will any more than we can force ourselves to love. The experience of Oneness comes to us without effort as we let go of our perceptions. It is possible to have this awareness all of the time if we are willing.

The Power of Desire

While *being* cannot be attained using our will, our efforts are important when one understands the power of desire and searching. The seeking of the Divine is effective because the desire for change brings it about. Seeking a change, we begin to release our present hold on what we call reality. Our efforts to attain Divine Reality by creating a concept of it does not work because our human minds, which are creating our current reality, cannot reach beyond the illusory level. If we were really human, Divine consciousness would be impossible, but we are merely pretending to be human while holding the Divine in us captive and hidden. Reality is released by our desire for something better, so it is our noninterference and not our actions that is effective. *Being* comes through Grace. *Being* awareness does not use the idea of positive thinking or imaging. Positive concepts are better than negative ones, but they do not have a lasting effect. These methods involve using the human mind to attain expanded awareness. While they do increase our awareness of our potential, they do not have the power to reach beyond the limitations of human consciousness. In short, they cannot reach beyond their own grasp.

Human minds catalog, retrieve, and postulate based only on current and past experiences. They are incapable of creating something new beyond the level of their experience. To reach a state of true awareness and vision, we must set the human mind aside and allow the Divine Mind, our only real Mind, to do the work. This Divine Mind is totally one with all knowledge and integrated with every facet of Creation. Thinking with this Mind requires no effort except the effort of not using your judgments, perceptions, and concepts to make decisions. As you begin to experience *being* consciousness, the limitation of human thinking is unmasked.

The Creative Aspects of Being

Creative breakthroughs come from inspiration, not perspiration. Everyone who has had a creative idea realizes, if he or she is honest, that it was not the result of their thinking. Creative ideas occur when human thinking and efforts are suspended. Creativity is an act of discovery. It is not really a *creation* of something but rather a *finding* of something. Creativity comes through new connections in which we move beyond the familiar where relationships are known, to an expanded level in which new relationships are discovered. To move beyond the known level into uncharted ground is the essence of creativity.

The creative function always goes beyond current reality to new possibilities. Often the strenuous efforts put into experimentation serve to create a situation in which the discoverer gives up his or her current concepts. This release clears away the old and opens the mind to new possibilities beyond its present perceptions. Many great discoveries are the result of a flash of recognition that occurred when the mind was open and willing to see a new relationship. It is interesting that as one discovers the new relationship, there is always a feeling of seeing the obvious.

The visual image of a light bulb going on represents creativity quite accurately. The creative idea bursts nearly fully grown upon the scene. It does not generate over a period of time, perfecting itself slowly. The creative idea suddenly occurs in one's mind and immediately answers the problem. The discoverer suddenly sees things fit together or recognizes the solution in a glance. It is an act of finding. It is not produced by the discoverer, but seems to have always been there waiting to be recognized. Often the discoverer has the feeling that he or she should have seen it before. It seems so simple and so right. After seeing the right solution, it is often impossible to think of any other solution. These same properties relate to the *listening* process, of which creativity is part.

Creativity is not a mental process. It is not the act of thinking about the problem and figuring out a good solution. The thinking process, while useful, is limited. The creative process will often change the seeming problem into an advantage or create such a different approach that the problem no longer exists. That is why it is so important that the *listening* process be coupled with the *accepting* process. Creativity is an act of inclusion and of seeing new relationships rather than rejecting them. The more judgment and criticism we use, the less open we are to *accepting,* which increases our awareness of relationships and opens us to new possibilities.

Why is all this important, and what does it have to do with *being?* Creativity is often the best way, particularly in the beginning, to experience *beingness.* To reach the *being* state, one must let go of personal effort and perceived needs. Like the creative idea, *beingness* appears when the time is right. Let me give you a simple example that may clarify what I'm talking about. It is important that you feel how it occurs so you can relate to it in terms of your own experience and feelings.

How Being *Feels*

I am sure you have had the experience of losing some object. Your first reaction, if you are like most of us, is to begin thinking about how you can solve the problem. Let's assume you have mislaid your car keys. Your mind begins to process something like this: When was the last time I remember seeing or using those keys? Where was I, and what was I wearing?

You search the pockets of these articles and look in places where you remember last having seen your keys. You may then begin to trace your movements forward to the present, looking around in all the places you have been. Never in this process do you go past the known. In fact, the known—where you were, what you did, and what you were wearing, is uppermost in your mind. You have used this thinking process before, and often it will be successful in finding your keys. It is not a bad process, but it is limited; in this case, the solution is limited to what you can remember.

Let's assume, however, that you fail this time. The next step is often taken but seldom recognized as an important step. You give up your effort to find the keys. This is not a mental exercise; it is an actual giving up. You may say, "If I find the keys, okay, but if I don't, I'll just get new ones made." Now you must stop thinking about the problem. If you can do this, often you will be given a creative solution. It may come in a moment or in a few hours, or it may take days, for it has its own timetable.

Here are several ways the solution can happen. The idea of where the keys are pops into your mind. You suddenly remember where they are and you find them. You may consciously or unconsciously look in a drawer and find the keys. You may be doing something else and find them. Someone else may find them and bring them to you.

An unlimited variety of things may happen, including the possibility that you do not find the keys but get some new ones made, and something good occurs because of that. This is the state of *being* concerning the lost keys. You allow your lack of concern to produce a satisfying result. *Being* is the state of allowing what will be to come about without interference. This willingness to remove all your energy and thought from a seeming problem often produces something wonderful. You can extend this *being* process to all aspects of your life.

The Doing and Being *Processes Contrasted*

The doing process is the opposite of *being*. It is not wrong or bad; in fact, doing often seems necessary while we are in the human dimension. However, unless one realizes its limitations, it can be quite frustrating. Let's examine how the doing process works. First, it outlines a plan of action that it thinks might work. This plan is fashioned from past experiences that seem relevant to the current problem. If the past experience has been successful and if the two situations are the same, then the repetition of the solution is usually successful. The difficulty begins if we do not realize that the situations are different or if we don't recognize that our past solution did not work. Even the assumption that there is a problem can be where those who rely solely on the doing process begin their erroneous actions.

At the human level, all of life is a problem to be solved, controlled, or avoided. Most of these problems we perceive as caused by others. This belief puts the solutions beyond our control and into other hands. Now someone else must change for us to be happy. Very often as we work on these perceived problems, they become more difficult and require greater effort. We often reach the *being* stage only after exhausting all other possibilities. It is always possible to release the idea that we know what should occur and allow what is, to be. Usually, however, it take a great deal of pain and stress for us to reach this release point. *Letting go,* which has become such a popular buzz phrase, is not a solution; it is merely the first necessary step we must take to reach objectivity. Only from a state of open-mindedness can we watch the situation clarify. Here, wholeness rather than blame, acceptance rather than control, and patience rather than force, are the hallmarks.

When I have reached this stage, which often takes some time, I begin to see that my "problem" is not a problem. Sometimes I only reach the place of beginning to question that I have a problem. That is enough. Now, rather than looking for a solution, I see that all is well. What was needed was not a change in the situation but a different perspective on my part of what was happening. Usually, this new perspective is much more inclusive.

At the doing level, my perspective is very personal. What are they doing to me, why are they doing it, and how can I make them stop? My judgment of what to do is based on how the situation affects me. At the *being* level, I begin to see what is happening as part of a larger picture. Not only how it affects me, but how it affects everyone, is important. Force and control are not helpful because all will do their part naturally. They may not do their part as I want them to do it, but they will do their part as best fits the whole picture. If I open my mind, I can begin to see that all is in harmony, and the situation is evolving naturally. At the doing level, the timetable is usually now. At the *being* level, the timetable is not as vital as everyone's peace and joy.

Change Is an Illusion

We have the notion that someday, due to our dedication and hard work, we will become enlightened and live a life of peace and joy. Many view our present life experience as a continuing process that teaches us what to do and how to act. Some extend this view to many lifetimes and see the process as learning right from wrong, helped along by punishment for our past mistakes. No matter how the concept is stated, it basically implies that we humans are in need of change and that in some way we should effect this change. This concept assumes that things are wrong and that a mistake occurred in the past that we need to correct. This false premise limited by the concept that change is necessary avoids ever looking to see if our judgment is flawed.

These may be helpful ways of thinking for a time, but they are not Reality. We are perfect now regardless of what we think. You may think of your experience as a dream or an illusion, and that is a pretty good description. However, this philosophy can create the concept that upon awakening, something very different happens. What really happens is that we are no longer trapped in our drama or restricted by our self-centered viewpoint. The truth is that this experience and everyone and everything in it is perfect—not as a perfect lesson or perfect punishment, but simply perfect.

What causes the pain, stress, and confusion is our limited concepts. These concepts reinterpret Reality and cause us to project our single-minded viewpoint upon everything. The effect of this is so strong that we literally create another reality based on our beliefs. We ignore what is and substitute in its place what we think is happening. This projection seems like Reality, but it is merely our projection. Its effects last only as long as our individual belief lasts. We then compound the situation further by thinking that we need to improve this false reality. That will never work. We will only create another false reality based on a new set of beliefs. Our only real need is to be aware of Reality. This can only take the form of not interfering with its unfoldment.

Reality Is Knowable Here and Now

To experience Reality, we must desire nothing else but
that. The hard part is that we have no idea what Reality is
or what it looks like. Thus, we must be willing to release
what we now experience as true for something that is
unknown. This is the leap of faith, the step into the
unknown, the open-minded trust to allow what is to
become evident. Do not underestimate the fear we all have
in taking this step. Because of this fear, we are gently led
in a series of easy steps. Even these small steps are usually
taken only when we have exhausted all other possibilities.
So this process may take a long, long time. The greatest
incentive to take these steps is the pain caused by the failure of our illusions. Be patient with yourself and others,
knowing that each awakening step comes at just the right
time. While awakening takes honesty and courage, all will
eventually welcome it. Awakening is simply the desire to
dream no more.

THE THREE AWARENESS THAT LEAD TO REALITY

The First Awareness Is Our Divine Connection

To begin this process of stepping into the unknown, we
need to realize that our minds merely interpret what we
experience. There is no reality in this knowing because it is

totally dictated by what we expect to perceive. Thus, we are, in a very real sense, the cause of our experiences. Perception is individual, the total product of the perceiver. While there are common experiences, no two people ever experience the situation in exactly the same way. While Truth does exist here, it will not be experienced until we shut down our minds, suspend our desire to understand, and simply *listen* to what is. I describe this process fully in my first book, ***Listening.*** The process of trusting our inner guide or inner voice instead of worldly voices and personal perception is usually a process of gradual release. It grows and grows as each individual experiences more peace and joy by *not* using their perception. Trust grows as we place less faith in our ability to figure things out, and place more faith in our inner guide or inner voice, which is our Divine Source.

We are so used to using our human mind to survive and succeed that in the beginning it often feels as if we are giving up all that we know. As we go beyond our mind, we begin to find a source of superior information. The more we use and rely on this source, the more this Divine Source becomes evident. When we trust that this inner guide is the best source of information all the time, we are ready for the next step.

The Second Awareness Is That Everything Is Helpful

Now, in addition to using our inner guide to choose the right path and to provide superior information, we begin to see that even before we ask, the way opens for us. We no longer need to ask what to do or how to choose, since we begin to find that all that comes to us is for our benefit. Now we ask not what to do, but how to see each situation properly. Do not misunderstand this step. I am not saying that everything that comes to us is what we want humanly. I am saying that no matter what situation comes to us—whether it seems good or bad in our judgment—it contains within it the possibility of a blessing. By using the *accepting* process, we no longer try to avoid or attract anything. What Divine Reality sends us is revealed as helpful. We ask our inner guide not *what* to do but for the correct interpretation of each event. *Accepting* is not using special perception to choose between concepts of good and bad, right and wrong, and just and unjust. Psychic powers or special insights may reveal the currently unknown, but they still require choosing which course is best. By *accepting,* we go beyond the need to choose because all is part of our spiritual awakening. My second book, ***Accepting,*** describes this process in detail. When we really trust that everything is a potential blessing and that our only need is for clarity, we are ready for the next step.

The Third Awareness Is That All Is One

Now we begin to see things clearly. From that clarity we look upon Reality. *There is not a desire to* **change** *anything including our self.* We do not need to *do* anything. That does not mean we are inactive, but that our activity comes without strain or special thought. We see everything as interrelated, and we are part of this natural harmony. We wait, knowing that what truly is will be revealed at the proper time. We may still see things that appear to be problems, but we know that they are merely problems of our vision. We quietly wait until our vision clears and the Truth appears. We never question what to do, for all that we need to do is to love. At times, when we are unsure what is loving, we simply turn within and ask. From that guidance, we act even if it does not match our concept of what is loving. If we are in doubt, we wait until clarity comes.

Being reveals our true spiritual identity. In the *being* state, we find that our present judgments, past experiences, and future needs are old concepts that have no basis in Reality. We can live totally in the present with no need to reference the past or future. We rest in a state of not giving thought to what we shall eat or wear, where we shall go, or who we shall be with. We trust the present to be all that is.

How Our Concepts Interfere with Being

Since we are deeply convinced that our worldly mind is our real mind, the *being* process may feel like letting go of all that we have attained and accomplished. The mere act of seeking to gain is sufficient to prevent the awareness of *being*. By searching for something, we never question the possibility that nothing is lost. The belief in loss precludes the possibility that Oneness is true. Nothing can be lost if all is one. *Being* does not look upon sickness, mistakes, or losses either in ourselves or others. It sees what appears, and not stopping there goes straight through the illusion to Truth. It dispels our perceptions and concepts and reveals the Reality they have hidden. We go past the desire to change or correct the illusion by knowing that all is well despite what we think. This is not avoidance of what seems to be, but a journey straight into the heart of the illusion. If we are trapped by an illusion and we need clarity, we *listen.*

It may seem strange that the way to vision is to admit we see the illusion. Trying to deny or avoid what you believe is real only gives it strength. We must be honest when we are deceived and not pretend all is well until we know it deep within our *being.* Every time we are deceived and feel that something is wrong, we ask again for clarity, and we wait for its appearance. While waiting, it may be helpful to remind yourself that you are willing to give up the concept that you see before you. When we can look upon the illusion and truly feel that nothing is wrong, we are free. You will know when this happens because the feeling of release and clarity is fantastic. Here's one of my personal experiences.

All Is God

For most of my life, I have had several growths under my arms. Recently on a lecture trip, one of them became quite inflamed. I tried for days to get a spiritual healing, but nothing worked. Believe me, I tried every technique I know. I finally went to a hospital emergency room to get the mole removed, but I was told that unless I stayed in town for several days so they could run tests, nothing could be done. My schedule did not permit such a delay. I continued on, hoping for a spiritual healing and trying to ignore the increasing pain. Finally, I decided that what will be, will be. I resolved to do nothing and accept the consequences. I even imagined that I might die of this growth. I continued with my activities and kept playing golf despite the pain. A week later after a golf game, I was walking by a pay phone when I was directed by my inner guide to look in the yellow pages for a clinic. I did so and found the name of one that sounded familiar. I called but feared they would also turn me away. Despite my fears of rejection, the nurse told me that she saw no problem removing it immediately. She gave me an appointment in one hour. I went to the clinic, which turned out to be some distance away, despite my doubts that I would be helped and in spite of my general dislike of medical facilities.

On the drive to the clinic, I was torn between the hope of having the growth removed and my desire to have a spiritual healing rather than a medical one. This desire was based on my long history of having spiritual healings and my feeling that they were the only real healings. My inner guide asked me as I drove along, "Would you go to the clinic if God was there?" "Of course," I answered. "What makes you think He is not there in the form of a doctor?" my inner guide responded.

I realized at that moment that all healings, in whatever form, are spiritual. When I arrived, I was taken almost immediately to the doctor's examining room. As I waited, I remembered that I was sweaty from playing golf. So I removed my shirt and began to wash under my arms. I looked down at the paper towel after I dried off and saw that the growth had come off in the cleaning process. I was amazed, elated, and relieved. For nearly a month, I had tried everything short of cutting it off myself, and until now my mole had resisted all efforts. As the doctor came in, I joked with him about his amazing clinic. "All one has to do here is just show up to get healed." I stated. He seemed delighted, also, and said he charged more for "miracles." The only cost to me was the release of my judgment about healings. As I drove back to my motel, I realized that it made no difference how the healing occurred, since every healing is spiritual.

My Concepts Limit My Awareness

Every concept I believe—no matter the content—limits me. In the example above, my belief that a spiritual healing was better than a medical one was a limiting concept. My concepts of myself as successful, capable, and smart; or my negative concepts of myself as unlovable, selfish, or unattractive are all limitations. Both positive and negative concepts limit us, although positive concepts may seem to be better. The truth is that none of us can be defined by a concept. Each concept becomes a small re-creation of myself that I must support. Once I identify with the concept, it defines all my actions. So if I have the concept that I am a spiritual searcher, then I can only be happy with a spiritual healing by a spiritual person. Can you see how this limits me? From the concept that I am a spiritual seeker, I define what is spiritual and what is not. I then eliminate all that I judge not spiritual and gravitate to what I think is spiritual—all the time ignoring the fundamental Truth that everything and everyone is spiritual.

We create concepts to support our individuality. They seem to work for a while by helping us define others and ourselves. Our present method of thinking requires concepts. We cannot stop making concepts. Even the concept of making no concepts is a concept. We simply realize that the thinking that creates concepts is not true. That is why *listening* is always necessary. *Listening* sees our concepts clearly and uses them to lead us to Reality. *Accepting* suspends our judgment, and judgment is the way we protect our concepts. These two processes lead us naturally to *being*, where we can release our concepts and experience Oneness.

*The
willingness to not
take your concept
seriously frees you
to <u>be</u>!*

CHAPTER 3

The Dark Night of the Soul

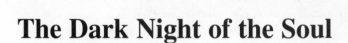

Willingness to Let My Concepts Die

Much has been written about this somber period in other people's lives, but I never believed that it was necessary in my own life—not until the winter of 1992 when I first wrote this chapter. Then I was very alone and right in the middle of this painful period. I could not reconcile the torment I felt then with the gentle process of returning to God that had been mine for the previous ten years. I was told that when this period was finished, it would place me on a higher level of awareness, but that was no comfort.

I have often pondered the Book of Job in the Bible. I even wrote a college essay about this man of God who was tested by Satan. I had always struggled with the reason why God allowed such a trial of one of His devoted followers. Now I feel that that story was a description of my soul's torment. At the time, I wondered if I could have avoided this trial in some way. Maybe this "test" occurs along the way to all serious seekers. Let me share it with you as I first wrote it.

> *As I tell you about this, it is a stormy day. The rain and my tears run together, and I feel as if there is nothing left for me. All that is Lee has been stripped away. I cannot rely on any concept of myself as a good person, a husband, a lover, a writer, a lecturer, or whatever. It is not that I am willing to release these concepts, but rather, every time I lean on them for any support, they vanish. I have nothing to hold on to and nowhere to go.*
>
> *I feel like a building with no foundation. It is very unpleasant and unnerving. There is a great deal of sadness connected with the loss of my persona. I have changed my concepts before, but I have always been able to replace them with improved versions. Now, every persona I try to identify with melts away. This happens in very strange ways. Let me give you an example.*

My Author Persona

> *For nearly 10 years, my self-published books have sold very well. In the last six months, several large pub-*

lishers have come to me and offered to publish and pro-
mote my books. At first, I was slightly interested but had
no real desire to become a famous author. I rather liked
my anonymity and the freedom it gave me to move about
on my own schedule. However, the more I thought about
wider distribution, the more it appealed to me. Having a
big firm publish my books would not only increase distri-
bution, but with someone else promoting my works I
would be freer to write and travel. Each time I explored
the issue and got excited about the prospects, the various
publishers, for one reason or another, decided not to
proceed.

When that happens, I become disappointed and
angry because when the offers are withdrawn, it seems
like rejection. There is a great temptation to protect
myself and to pretend I don't care. But I do care, and I am
hurt. I am especially angry at the process that presents
something to me, attracts me to it, and then snatches it
away. This has been happening over and over in every
facet of my life. The whole process takes on the substance
of vapors and clouds, creating objects that when touched
have no solidity. It occurs to me, as I describe what has
been happening, that this process helps define my con-
flicted desires—desires that I have but which I repress
because they are in conflict with some of my other desires.
I do not like this process on any level. I want to believe I
am all right since it is part of my spiritual path, but deep
down I feel abused.

My Preference Is to Avoid Pain

I prefer my spiritual path to move gently and lovingly forward and upward, bringing with it new vistas and increased joys. The current painful process does not match my pictures of what a spiritual quest should be. Yet on a very deep level, I am aware that this process, called the "dark night of the soul," is very necessary. Without it I would not be able to look at my deeply hidden, secretly cherished, but conflicted beliefs. Take the publishing rejection, for example. I desire to have my books read and to receive recognition for my part in their manifestation. On the other hand, I like my privacy and hate to promote myself. These attitudes seem in conflict.

What I do with conflicting desires is to try to reconcile them or avoid looking at them. To date, I have been willing to acknowledge my visible desires for love and acceptance and offer them up for correction. What I have problems with are my hidden desires, such as a need for fame and success. The very act of hiding them from myself confirms that I don't wish to look at them. To offer them for correction, I must first realize that I have these desires. I have hidden these desires because these parts of me are not appealing. What has been happening is that these parts that represent my hidden desires are revealed to me through pain. When the pain of rejection occurs, for example, I am shown that my desire for more recognition or even fame cannot be hidden any longer.

Hidden Self-Concepts

For me, the difficult part of this process is not to become defensive. I have a great desire to protect myself. This persona I want to protect is not me, but a jumbled combination of concepts about who I am. My normal reaction to challenges to my hidden concepts is to ignore the challenge and avoid future situations that might cause them to surface. I know that once the hidden desire comes to my attention, I leave myself open to disappointment. In short, I am afraid of my easily hurt vulnerability. Over and over, I have been shown that as I am willing to be vulnerable in a strange, wonderful way, I become invulnerable. I have learned that hiding my concepts from my awareness causes the pain and stress.

I have been amazed by how well being honest with myself works, even though I usually only view it in retrospect. Each challenge to my vulnerability need not be automatically met on my part by a defensive reaction. I can stop this knee-jerk conditioning. I have tried all my life to become invulnerable. I have tried to strengthen myself, become more placid, and to be the first one to reject a situation. Now, I am being asked by my inner guidance to be willing to be rejected. In this rejection and the pain that follows, I get a clear understanding of what is being rejected. It is not the real me that is ever being rejected. It is always a concept I hold about myself. When I recognize the concept as not meaningful, then I am no longer hurt by its appearance. When someone's actions reveal a concept such as a desire for recognition, I realize that it is only an idea I hold about me, and that it is not me.

When my hidden concept of myself as famous writer is rejected, I can see clearly that I have a great investment in the concept of myself as a writer. I am surprised, because on one level I have no desire to be a great writer, yet on another level I do have a deep desire to be loved. I keep these desires separated so I do not have to reconcile them. When my conflicting self-concepts are revealed, rather than deny the discrepancy, I simply need to ask for clarity. I need to open to new ways of being, and remember that while I am happy as an author, I am also willing to be something else. Can you see why the question, "What do I really want?" is so important? This question helps clarify any conflicting self-concepts and focuses my awareness on what is currently true for me. What work I do is just a temporary expression of who I am, and not my real being.

I must be willing to give up the concept of myself as the independent self-published writer or even the concept of being an author. The truth is that neither concept is who I am. I am always my being regardless of the manifestation I am currently using to represent me. When I can see that my hidden, conflicting desires are not maintaining my concept, I must not rush to create another concept that works better. My real freedom comes as I realize that no concept will ever be sufficient to satisfy me. What a challenge to be willing to let go of my self-concepts! That is very different from me trying to change them. As I let this be done, there is no real feeling of completion—only *a continuum of change. This lack of solidity that I must not seek to make more comfortable is the blank space on which my real being begins to manifest. Being, as I now experience it, is not the rejection of self-concepts, but a state of nonattachment to them.*

During this roller-coaster process of revelation, my part is not to become attached to the momentary events. I need to meditate and be still often to get clarity on what is happening. Sometimes I am only able to calm my fears, but I cannot move past them. My desires and plans rush at me and tempt me to take action to draw something or someone to me. I feel a great need mentally and physically to grab on to something solid, but there is nothing solid here. My connection with the Divine is not sufficient to feel totally supported. My attachment with my former solid concepts has been shattered. So I'm feeling very adrift and disconnected somewhere between the human and the Divine, with no solid connection to either in my awareness.

The Opposite of What We Think

Today, great emphasis is put on being a successful person. Many spiritual self-help programs are built around the concept of using spiritual truths to achieve wealth, power, and recognition. That is the opposite of what I believe really works. As the humanness within us dies, it is then that our true spiritual *being* comes forth.

I am reminded of the Beatitudes in the Bible. Blessed are the meek, and blessed are the poor in spirit. Meekness and poverty of spirit are attitudes that lessen the persona or personal sense. It is only as our concept of humanness is diminished that our real *being* can manifest. Since it is the Divine *Being* that gives us life and works through us, the human being must be relinquished for our real *being* to emerge. This rejection and failure of our persona is not something the human part of us *wants* to do or even *can* do. As each human concept about us fails, which it always does, we must allow it to slip away. The key is not to replace it with something else. This process feels like total vulnerability and, at times, even a personal death. As human beings, we try to survive by becoming invulnerable to challenges through a response of attack or defense. When these defenses and attacks are given up, the first realization is one of nakedness and lack of substance. All that seemed to protect us in the past is gone. Thus, the meek and the poor in spirit—those not seeking to become successful human beings—are much closer to *being* than the much admired successful human.

The Blank Space

A blank space where little persona is present is the exact condition needed for the emergence of our spiritual *being*. Our connection with the Divine is always there unchanged, but it is hidden behind the persona we create.

The spiritual *being* is visible only to the extent the human being is not seen. The dark night of the soul is the activity in which the release of the human persona is accomplished. It feels very lonely and is filled with uncertainty because no other human can join us in the process. Even my inner guide who was so present during the beginning of my journey seemed whimsical and uncertain during this time.

In the beginning of our conscious spiritual journey, inner guidance feels powerful. We see clarity and direction coming from our inner guide, and it brings us all we need. We learn we are better cared for by our inner guidance than by our own planning processes. This happy period creates such a reliance on our spiritual source that it is impossible for us to return to our former ways.

There comes a time, however, when the journey is less certain. As we give up the idea that we know where we are going, the companion idea that we do not know who we are or where we are going begins to dawn on our consciousness. On the spiritual path, as each step unfolds, we become more aware that we do not know the next step, let alone the direction the path is following. As our spiritual vision increases, our human vision becomes less accurate. Often our way does not lead where our human concepts of a spiritual journey point. We are cared for, but we cannot match this care to our perceived needs.

The Betrayal of Our Concepts

During my period of trial, I had just enough clarity concerning events to understand what was happening in the moment and an inkling of how it was useful to me. The problem began when I tried to match what *was* happening with what I thought *should* be happening. The biggest test came when my wife decided to leave our marriage of five years. All I had ever desired in my life was to share it with a loving companion. We met the first year I owned and ran Las Brisas Retreat Center. She did workshops that teach proper diet using inner awareness as the key. Even though I had been single for more than ten years and had no intention of entering into a marriage, we recognized each other as kindred souls and immediately joined our lives together. We ran the retreat center together, and it provided a wonderful environment for both our workshops.

Then, suddenly, she no longer wanted to be with me. Her needs and desires no longer matched mine. What I had wanted to make permanent and thought I could depend upon was gone in a few days. I was angry at the loss, angry at my ex-wife for what I thought was betrayal, but most of all angry at God who I knew had set the whole thing up. For many weeks, I could barely cope with life. I begged God to tell me why this was happening. Why was I being abandoned? Finally, the answer came as I was jogging, a method I have often used to make contact with guidance when I am very upset. I heard, "Lee, when will you give up the idea you can be abandoned? Every relationship you have ever experienced and every relationship you will ever have is only with me. I change form, but I will never leave you." That was very helpful, but it was fully a year before I had full peace with the situation, so deep were my fears of abandonment.

As much as I have feared betrayal and longed for loyalty in my life, it has eluded me. As you may know, if you have read my other books, I believe our core issues are hidden by our personal concepts. These core issues come to our spiritual awareness as we are ready to outgrow them. In the book, *Listening*, my core issue was my self-worth. I learned by following inner guidance in all things that I was lovable and I did not have to earn or do something to get it. In the book, *Accepting*, my core issue was competency. I learned that I did not have to prove my ability. Competency was a non-issue and merely a matter of someone's judgment. I also learned that everything that happened to me— even disasters—had the potential of becoming blessings. In this book, *Being*, I learned that I cannot be betrayed. I am one with all creation and therefore can never be separated. In Reality, everyone and everything is connected and therefore part of me.

Betrayal Unmasked

I got my total peace with betrayal in 1993 while talking with a good friend in New York. We were sharing our experiences with God's wonderful care, and as she spoke to me, I heard a voice in my inner ear. It said, "I was betrayed." I identified the voice as Jesus and acknowledged that I knew about Judas and his betrayal. "Not just Judas," said the voice. "Everyone betrayed me." I remembered that Peter denied Christ and that many of his followers ran and hid in fear during the time of his trial and execution. Still deep in my own self-pity from my betrayal, I felt the pain and loneliness I thought Jesus must have felt. Then the voice said, "The reason you have had issues with loyalty in your life is because you are a betrayer."

I would like to think that if I had been one of the disciples, I would have been willing to stand up and not be afraid. Yet, I am sure, like the others that I would have hidden and maybe even denied the Christ. I acknowledged that to this voice inside my head. I also realized at that moment that many people in my life probably felt I had betrayed them. My daughter and my first wife came to mind. Wow! Now I was really feeling bad. Then the voice said, "Many people thought I betrayed them. Don't feel bad. All human beings are betrayers. Do you know what a betrayer is, Lee?" Before I could answer, he said, "When someone doesn't do what we want them to do." The light dawned. No one had ever betrayed me; they all did exactly what they were supposed to do. Clarity came to me like a bolt of light. All that really happens when I feel betrayed is that my plans for others do not go according to my desires. Thus, I can never be betrayed; all that is betrayed are my plans for everyone. I can never betray others; all I can do is not fulfill their desires.

On a human level, we are all betrayers because we each have different needs, desires, and plans. Whenever we do not do what others have planned for us, whenever we disappoint, and whenever we take a course that others do not agree with on some level, they feel betrayal. When we do what others want us to do, we are deemed loyal even if it betrays our own deep convictions. It may seem a harsh definition, but it is true. No one in this world can go through an active life without causing others to feel betrayed by their actions. The only way to avoid the feeling of betrayal is to love everyone unconditionally. That means we love others without any plans, desires, or conditions about our giving of love.

Can you see that loyalty and betrayal are merely perceptions? What one group calls betrayal the opposing group might call loyalty. The choice is made not based on the actions of the person, but the group's perceived needs. Thus, concepts such as loyalty and betrayal, which seem sacred, are always subject to change. Eventually, the desire to be loyal and do what others expect, comes in conflict with one's own personal needs and desires. Even if we are following our inner guidance, the other person may feel betrayed. Betrayal is a perception caused by another's beliefs.

I cannot tell you the relief that poured over me with this revelation. I continued on my journey feeling great freedom from this limiting idea of betrayal. When a car almost smashed into me at an intersection an hour later, I was still so filled with joy that I motioned with a matador flourish for the car to proceed. I am not sure that the other driver's reaction was the same as mine, but no matter. I loved it. I got lost trying to bypass New York City. No matter. I enjoyed every magic minute as I drove round and round lakes and small villages in the autumn foliage.

Then I had lunch in a rustic diner and was served by a very salty waitress. I relished the quaint experience totally. It was several days before the flush of this wonderful revelation subsided. Even in retelling it, my love for all involved and the joy and freedom this awareness gives me returns. My sadness, which I thought was caused by betrayal, was the result of my disappointment in not getting my way.

Betrayal Is a Non-Issue

How, then, do we solve this betrayal/loyalty question? Simply, we do not react to others based on our perceptions and desires. We follow inner guidance and use that as the basis of our response. If we are willing to release our plans, or have plans we can change, it is impossible that we can be betrayed. At the spiritual level, we are integrated, and from this higher perspective, all is united. The issues of loyalty and individual needs do not actually exist. On the human level, this might be called a win/win situation. On the spiritual level, it is called Oneness. Only your inner guide can direct you on a path that is loving for all concerned.

Everything on earth eventually betrays us, whether it is our strength, our beauty, our intelligence, our health, or the persons we love. At some point in human existence, we are all faced with a situation in which one of our plans fails. We are confronted with our human limitations and frailty. Despite all our attempts to avoid this eventual failure of our concepts, it happens. They fail because they are not eternal but merely mortal. As you will see, this is wonderful, because as a result, we find we are not human, but spiritual, *beings*. If we were more successful perpetuating our humanness, we would never learn that we are more than mortal. Every concept that we create about our self as an intelligent, beautiful, or healthy person, or even as a spiritual and compassionate being, is a limitation on our Reality. The spiritual truth about us cannot be contained within the confines of our concepts. The only thing that does not betray us is our Divine Reality, which is unchanging.

Ending the "Dark Night of the Soul"

The "dark night of the soul" ends when we realize that our personal concepts are merely self-imposed limitations. This is true especially when it concerns our good concepts. The last effort we make in retaining our humanness is a reluctant release of loved ones, letting them do what they must do. When they do not support our individual desires or no longer remain close to us, we feel they have betrayed us. In reality, by their not doing as we wish, they give us the greatest gift. Through this gift, we realize that our concepts of being a loving companion, a caretaker, a provider, or a supporter—when used as our identity—is a limitation. Although it may appear to be a limitation on the other person, it is really and most of all a limitation on our self. In freeing and continuing to love unconditionally, we find our own freedom. Like the bird pushed from the nest, we learn to be free of restraining concepts and fly. Now we are truly free. Let us examine another attribute that flows to us in this transformation.

CHAPTER 4

Peace Beyond Understanding

Survival in a Dangerous World

*L*istening to a higher source not only provides us with a source of clarity, it also quiets the human mind. This so-called mind is basically concerned with our survival and safety. It spends its time planning and protecting us. Its basic premise is that we are living in a world of danger and conflict. It believes that only careful planning and aggressive action can prevent our demise. We seldom question this premise. The vast majority of the world's thinking revolves around a constant concern for safety. What we call thinking is mostly worrying about the future. While we claim that living in a world of conflict is stressful, I find few people who would really like to be peaceful all the time. They dislike conflict and worry but find the struggle both exciting and motivational. They believe that some pain and pressure is necessary for progress. Must we continue a cycle of pleasure and pain, joy and sorrow, achievement and disappointment, without ever considering if this is necessary? Do we have a great stake in maintaining conflict? Yes, because this conflict provides the glue that holds our deeply held belief in duality together.

Duality Keeps Us Trapped

Duality is the concept of two alternatives, two powers, or two possibilities. In this life, we often feel the full effect of events by contrast. So without sorrow, could we know joy? Without failure, could we know the thrill of success? The belief in the presence of two powers—even those as basic as good and evil—seems to be necessary to support our present reality. If there was only good or only evil, how could we differentiate? If, for example, there was only chaos, chaos would be our normal experience. We would not dislike it because we would be unaware of any other possibility. Total lack of order would be the only possibility, and we would never expect things to follow a logical pattern. We would expect, live with, and find chaos normal. Being used to chaos if we suddenly had to deal with order might be unnerving. Can you see that the possibility of an opposite is what creates lack of peace? It is the possibility of an "other," not order or chaos, which creates conflict. The idea that something else besides the expected can happen causes us all our worry. That is why people avoid the unknown even when the known is very unpleasant. In this world, which is based on the illusion of two or more possibilities, we are required to choose which we want and then seek to attain it. This keeps us always searching and always in a state of concern about the future. With only one possibility and therefore no need for choice, peace would have to be our state of mind. No choice means there is no conflict. At present, our use of free will is limited to making choices within this illusion of life. These choices are not real choices, but only illusions of choice.

The Knowledge of Good and Evil

The biblical story of the Garden of Eden is a mythical representation of this duality. Adam and Eve had to leave heaven because they ate the fruit of the tree of the knowledge of good and evil. I always wondered why it was the tree of good "and" evil. Why not just the tree of evil? In the myth, the idea of ingesting the apple is a symbol for taking duality into one's consciousness. The problem caused by the knowledge of good and evil was not simply the recognition of evil, but the necessity of choice caused by the introduction of this dualistic idea. The "need" to choose and the idea that humans could make meaningful choices ensnared Adam and Eve. This is the great lie of the serpent in the allegory. He stated that to eat of this fruit was to become as a god, knowing both good and evil. Judgment is always reserved for God throughout the Bible in both the Old and New Testaments. That is because only in a fully aware Divine State can judgment be looked upon and seen as unreal. It is interesting that Adam and Eve were not conscious of choice until they ate the forbidden fruit.

Once they ate of the fruit, they realized that they were naked. When they realized they were naked, they needed to hide and cover up their natural state. In their naked state, Adam and Eve were happy. There was nothing to hide and nothing to cover up. They did not know they were naked because they did not know of any other possibility. Once they thought about even two simple possibilities, being naked or clothed, they had to choose. In this case, they renounced their natural state and decided to add something. It is stated that they added a covering because they felt ashamed. This is a good analogy for how we create our human concepts and use them to cover up our true nature and hide our true self.

From here on, all sorts of choices opened up. Adam and Eve were cast out of the Garden of Eden—a state in which no choices existed—by the need to make judgments. Can you see from this little story that a natural, peaceful, or heavenly state results when there is no other possibility? This is the peace of Oneness. This peace cannot be reached by trying to make good judgments; it only comes when we desire no other possibility. This is the state of *being*. It is the result of giving up judgment, a power that we do not really have. Judgment is reserved for God because there is nothing to judge.

Going back to the story, Adam and Eve broke the Commandment not to eat the fruit of the tree of the knowledge of good and evil and were faced with a new viewpoint that forced them into a world of conflict, pain, and toil. If there were really two powers, there would be no way for us, the descendants of Adam and Eve, to return to Heaven. I am aware of some of the popular beliefs concerning how mortals can get into heaven. One theory is that by doing good works and through a process of learning from our mistakes, in time we will be granted admission. Some theories state it takes many lifetimes, and some speculate that all negative acts must be redeemed by good acts. Another theory states that given a sacrifice or atonement, God will be appeased for our transgressions and allow us to return. Both of these ideas have many variations.

Frankly, their rationale never satisfied me when I was in my early teens, and they still lack credibility today. I believe there is a better way, a more direct approach to this search for Heaven. We can simply accept the first account of Creation. God created everything, and behold, it was very good. Thus, Creation is perfect, now and forever. Nothing can ever go wrong because there is no choice in Reality, and our only need is to be aware of Reality.

Choice in the Illusion

We are created in God's image and likeness. Like God, we have free will. In Reality, this free will is the power to create. In the human state, it becomes the power to choose. We can use our will to choose the illusion of an existence apart from God. Since we are always part of God, we cannot exist in what is unlike Creation except in illusion or dreams. Reality and Oneness preclude any part of Creation being different or separate.

In duality, there is always conflict because there are opposites. In the dream, we use duality to feel separate from the Creator and to experience our own indivi-"duality." We do not hate duality, despite the fact that our illusory creation has brought us effects we do not like and cannot control. It serves our purpose by fostering our desire to be individual. We also created the concept of others who are separate from us, with different needs and desires. That is why the idea of peace does not attract us except as a temporary respite from the stress and pain that always accompanies our attempts to be separate. To achieve peace requires nothing on our part. Peace, harmony, and happiness, our natural birthrights, come to us whenever we stop interfering with Creation's Oneness. We do this when we see our brothers' and sisters' needs as one with ours and when we choose not to be separate from them.

We should not find it difficult to release conflicting desires and be still. It takes constant mental effort to support separation. We do not experience separation as effort but rather as worry and concern about our safety and well-being. When we release this concern, which is based on the false assumption that we are vulnerable, we experience peace even in the midst of others experiencing stress and conflict. If we realize our true Oneness, vulnerability is impossible. This is the peace beyond understanding.

The Need to Understand Traps Us

Trying to understand is an illusion that leads us deeper and deeper into the maze. There is nothing in the illusion of individuality to understand. The solution is simple. In the midst of stress and conflict, create a blank space of non-judgment. This idea runs counter to everything that our mind is telling us to do. *Accepting* is the only solution that works, but it is usually the last one we choose. *Accepting* is not resignation; it is being still and releasing all ideas of conflict. Seeking to understand a situation gives it all the reality it has. When we withdraw our support in the form of fear or understanding from any stressful situation, it no longer has power. Now with our mind still and open, peace will come of its own volition. If there is something to do, we will be gently led to do it, and it will be easily accomplished.

If we try to use our minds to create peace, we will only create an illusion of peace, which is temporary and not satisfying. Illusory peace requires special conditions such as beautiful vistas, quiet settings, and loving friends. Real peace is not of our doing; it has no conditions and can come to us in any situation. We do not draw peace to us; it was always there. You will wonder how you could have ever become so involved in the turmoil when you see that peace is so easily available.

Give up the idea that your understanding is helpful. Your human mind is what seeks to understand. This is not a real mind, but a process of recalling past experiences, placing them in an order that seems to make sense, and then measuring the new experiences against this library of misinformation. Looked at honestly, this mind can be seen as constantly concerned with its own needs and desires and totally unaware of its connectedness. It judges everything in terms of what it will do for me. This me is not the real me, but a concept of who we are and what we need.

Judgment Keeps Us at the Level of the Problem

Our judgment cannot raise higher than its own concepts, so nothing new ever happens when we rely on it. Is it any wonder that our lives tend to be repetitions of past experiences, with new partners and new surroundings? To bring new experiences, we must access our unlimited mind. This is only possible when we realize that our limited mind does not understand anything. Realizing this, we can do nothing but voluntarily still this so-called mind. When our limited mind is truly still, so that it does not intrude with various solutions and plans, then our unlimited mind rushes to fill the void.

Our limited concept of who we are will never satisfy us. Being limited, for an unlimited *being,* is ultimately impossible. Being limited is, at best, temporary. Like a butterfly emerging from a cocoon, we will begin to emerge to freedom. It is not helpful to force this transformation which, by its nature, is gentle and graceful. It may take some time, but the period of transformation lasts only as long as we cling to familiar dreams.

Being *Brings Freedom to All*

Allow this *being* within you to emerge, and welcome its birth in your awareness. Going back is impossible even though some hopes may linger in a bittersweet fantasy of what you think could have been. It never could. Be grateful for the loss of each limited fantasy you experienced along the way, and thank those who played their part in bringing about the destruction. Your partners did not fail or betray you, but played their roles perfectly. It was not your friend that betrayed you, but the limited dream you placed them in. They, like you, drew great blessings from the encounter, brief or otherwise. Each person did their part as you did yours. All concerned moved closer to the awakening of the unlimited. No matter how painful, it was only painful enough to serve the purpose. The continued pain comes from your fantasy of how it should have been—not from the reality of how it was. These fantasies of what else might have been are our creations, and we need to let them go in the light of Truth.

All involved did the best they could, gave the maximum of love, and moved on at just the right time. It was your plan for limitation that failed—not God's plan for your awakening. Your plan involved only your personal needs. God's plan, in which you have an active and important part, involves everyone's unlimited joy and happiness. Knowing this, do you still want your plan to work? Knowing this, can you not look again on what happened and be at peace? Once we truly accept this truth, that God's plan is the best plan, we are capable of internal peace—a peace beyond any need to understand.

Replacing Good Concepts

The shocking news is that every concept we create, including those we call good, fails. Most people enter into a spiritual search, not to find out who they really are, but to find a way to create better concepts about themselves. It is quite a shock when these good concepts also fail, and it takes willingness to realize that no worldly concept is worthy of us. At first, we may believe that only the elimination of our negative concepts such as selfishness, greed, fear, hatred, or lust is required. Having done this, we are surprised when we do not find ourselves at peace. We can become discouraged when we don't get the approval and appreciation we now feel entitled to as a result of our efforts. The next step, which requires great courage, is to give up our good concepts. We usually do this only when our efforts to be loving, generous, and helpful fail not only others but ourselves. Now, no matter what we do, it seems not to work. We finally come to the point of not knowing what to do. Hopefully we can come to this point gratefully. We need to be willing to let the Divine manifest through us, and this willingness usually happens through a series of failures. Willingness means to release all doing, all thought of doing, and even the desire to do. The Divine *Being* within us must do the works. Only this brings peace and joy. Peace happens when we cease doing, still our desires, and allow the spirit that flows through us naturally to manifest.

Activity and Being

In the beginning, this state may seem quite unnatural. You will find yourself thinking, Surely there is something more I must do. The word *must* is a dead giveaway. When the Divine *Being*, the *I am,* is doing the work, everything happens without thought or effort. Your activity unfolds easily. This is your normal state. It is natural for you to be doing something you love and something that is easy and joyful. Think what happens when you are doing something you truly love. The time passes quickly, the effort is easy, you have limitless energy, and joy flows through you, manifesting in wonderful ways. Your works flow out to others, touching them more deeply than you could ever imagine.

The key questions to ask yourself are, "Do I love to do this?" or "Do I feel I need to do this?" Feeling a need to do something may be very subtle. For example, I may feel I love to do something, but really I need to do it to get approval and love. I don't love what I am doing for the joy of doing it, but I love getting approval, which I think I need. The question, "Do I love to do this?" contains the concept of not getting anything in return. So you can ask yourself, "Would I do this if nothing came of it?" Now the focus is on the joy of *being,* not on the outcome. At this level, fatigue, stress, and disappointment are impossible. If you feel any disappointment, you can be sure that you, and not your *being,* are doing the work. So let's change the old saying, "No pain, no gain," until it becomes "No joy, no gain."

Freedom from Need

As you proceed to live, letting the Divine manifest through you, a sense of peace and freedom will grow within you. Outcomes now become unimportant. The Divine is doing what needs to be done, and it will be as it is meant to be. You may see much that you think needs to be done, but need is the concept that makes duality seem real. It is very helpful to continue to affirm that there is no need in Reality for my self or any part of creation. I do not need love, truth, abundance, or health. These are all part of my *being* and the *being* of everyone. These qualities were given to all of us in our creation. They flow to and through us as part of the Divine Will. Nothing we can do has any power to increase or decrease these attributes. To allow the Divine *Being* to flow through us to everyone and from everything back to us, we need only *listen, accept,* and *be.*

*Our real
power comes from
our willingness
to be a
transparency
for the Divine.*

CHAPTER 5

Being Present

At First, Frustration

Since I started my inner spiritual journey, I have been
given a few opportunities to touch the Divine for a
moment. In that state, I am always in awe, which, as I stated in the beginning of this book, is one of the similarities
our Divine nature has with our human consciousness. The
feelings of simplicity, order, and beauty I experienced in
this state were unique. These periods usually lasted for
only a few hours, sometimes far less. Despite my deep
desire to capture all the details, when they were over, little
remained, and it is difficult to describe in words what happened. What is always present and always remembered
was a great longing to return to that state.

When I was told by my inner guide that my next process was *being,* I felt that some grand breakthrough awaited me. I hoped these random Divine occurrences would now be attainable on a more permanent basis. I looked for something startling to happen. Quite some time passed before it occurred to me that *being* was not unique, but natural. Even though it was entirely beyond my control to call these experiences forth, I could sharpen my awareness of when they were happening. I began to see small glimpses of these occurrences happening frequently during the day—for example, when I felt compassion for or attunement with someone. The more I try to attain this state, the more it eludes me. The more I await its arrival, the more it happens. The only activity I can undertake that seems to bring *being* about is to release all my concepts of everything, including my concept of spirituality. Instead of using my head to figure things out, I can use my heart to join with whatever is around me and try to connect from a oneness perspective.

The *being* experience has been nearly the opposite of what I suspected it would be. *Being* started when all that I most desired was stripped away. It has continued with me, often *being* where I did not feel I am to be. I have felt more disconnected with the world around me during this time of Oneness than I have felt connected. I have felt very alone during a period when I longed to experience more Love. My strenuous efforts to find my proper place and expression did not begin to materialize until this final year of finishing this book. Nearly five years went by before I found my peace with it. The great breakthrough of *being* for most of the time felt more like frustration than joy. I believe the process felt this way because it involved the restructuring of my viewpoint. A whole new way of relating to things had to come about. The change of perspective went from "How does this affect me?" to "How do I relate to this?" Joining with what was happening was not always pleasant, since it involved giving up my control over what I thought I needed.

The First Commandment Revealed

Recently, in a meditation borne mostly from frustration with the world's unjust treatment, a new awareness dawned upon me. I had been told as a child to seek God first, and all else I needed would be supplied. I assumed that if I was a good person I would be taken care of by God and be given what would make me happy. I have known—forever, it seems—that the First Commandment is to love God. My childhood view had changed little over the years. I thought God wanted or needed my love. If I loved God, then I would get love in return. "NO!" was the answer. God does not need your love; God is love. God is not wanting to be loved, but *is* Love, the total essence, the total expression. As part of Creation, we are Love, also. We do not need Love; we *are* Love. As Love, we must express and manifest it as God does. Expressing it, we come to know that we have it.

I need to see what Love I can give today. I need to fully feel Love streaming out from me and surrounding me. This inclusion has been the essence of all my Divine experiences. I have been, at those wonderful times, totally present in the momentary feeling and at that instant connected with everything in a new way. I cannot feel connected with what is now while I worry about the past or the future. It dawned on me that was truly *being*. Not some mystical event, not some unworldly feeling, but total presence as I relate to all else. To do this, to *be* totally present and express Love, requires dropping all my concerns and all my worried thoughts. Worry and concern are not about the present. Worry is either past or future. If I am caught up in what is Loving now, it is impossible to worry. When I love what is now, as it is now, it is not hard to be happy.

Daily Bread

That is the beauty of the Bible references to daily bread, which means living the moment fully. At the time of Moses, the Jewish people, who wandered in the desert for 40 years, found that they could not store up the manna that fed them, but had to gather it each morning. Throughout recorded spiritual history, there is a theme of daily supply, staying in the moment and not hoarding. The idea of daily bread occurs again in the Lord's prayer given us by Jesus Christ: "Give us this day our daily bread." There is no need to store up or worry when we adopt the idea of moment-by-moment supply. Most people miss the point of abundance because they equate it with protecting resources. Once we undertake to store up, we give up the moment and look to the future. We become worried and see ourselves as the only source of supply, rather than looking to the Divine. Planning for coming events, we give up the current moments of joy for hope of joy in the future. Thus, moment by moment, we miss what is. Living this way, we pass up each golden opportunity and do not fully experience the present because of concern for something else. Future and past living is never fulfilling, since past remembrances and future hopes will never be as nourishing as current joy.

Is *being* really that simple? Just to be fully present. Yes. Looking back, I am sure that most of us can remember a situation that we desperately desired to leave. Now, in retrospect, that situation looks much more pleasurable, and we wonder why we were in such a hurry to move on. The best use of the *past* is the remembrance of our lack of willingness to be present in it when it was *now*.

The Value of Immediate Gratification

I love to travel. Early on in my explorations, I became aware that I would pass up the chance to fully enjoy the place I was in and rush to get to the next destination. It took a good deal of discipline to put my thoughts of tomorrow away so I could take in all that was present that day. It was difficult in my travels, but it is much more difficult in my ordinary life. When I am confronted with an unpleasant task, it is very hard to suppress the desire to get on to something I like. Many people spend the majority of their time rushing past the present and looking for the future. We can only stay in the present moment by moment. Doing this, we need not ask what to do; we merely do what is in front of us. If you do this and attend to the present, you will be amazed how quickly tasks are accomplished—even the unpleasant ones.

The chase for future happiness causes us to speed up our activity to the point where we are never really present. Rushing from one thing to another, we lose our awareness of what is real in our lives. If we still our minds, much the same as we do *listening* to our inner guide, we will find a richness around us that is very satisfying. Heaven is not far away; it can be reached by opening our eyes and stretching out our hands. How can we ever hope to reach awareness, in the spiritual sense, when we are not aware now in the physical sense? Looking to the future can blind us to the joy and beauty that is right next to us.

Speed, noise, worry, and the desire for something else all work to keep us blind and deaf to what would naturally leap into our consciousness and fill us with joy. Don't you always find more beauty and truth when you look deeply into something and get to know it? This is especially true of people. Doesn't greater appreciation of others always follow understanding and awareness? Isn't love the natural outcome of fully seeing? How often have we rushed by what we seek? Maybe our quest for future delights is a good way to avoid present joy.

Awareness Is Always in the Moment

One thing I have struggled with all my life is my weight. I am trying to be more aware of what I am eating at the present. I am endeavoring to take my time as much as possible with each bite. I try to prepare my food with care and awareness and place it on the plate in a pleasing manner. I am learning to taste each morsel and pause between mouthfuls. I am trying to be aware of when I am full, by stopping occasionally to feel my body and see if it is satisfied. While I have not completed this process, I am seeing a gradual loss of excess weight and an increase in my enjoyment of meals. If I am eating something only because it tastes good and not because I am hungry, I stop and place the remainder in a plastic bag so I can enjoy it later. I resist the temptation to clean my plate, which keeps me from being aware of how I feel.

I know this technique of awareness will work. I'm sure it can be used in all areas of our lives. I am totally convinced that honest awareness is all that we ever need. We would know exactly what to do if we could remain honestly aware in all situations. Awareness is not figuring things out, but merely becoming an observer of what is happening. We are capable of making poor decisions by going unconscious and reacting from deep-seated fears and anxieties. Thus, we never see what is going on and cannot place it in its proper perspective. When we take time to honestly look at each situation from a neutral position of awareness and clarity, we immediately call upon the Divine *Being* within us. This Divine part immediately emerges when we do not interfere. Our interference can be the result of unconscious distraction, as well as conscious resistance. Maybe this is a good place to stress the importance of being honest with yourself. A regular checkup of your thinking and your actions to be sure they represent the integrity you desire is always helpful.

Searching versus Being

Another way we lose awareness of the present is by constantly searching. Searching is based on the assumption that what is present is not enough and that something better is available. No one could be a more compulsive searcher than myself. For most of my life, my search for answers and better solutions was a double-edged sword. My searching formed the groundwork for my creativity and also for my constant dissatisfaction with everything. I am sure that it was the spark that brought my spiritual path to life.

It is not easy to face the state at which I find myself. I am ready to give up searching—not because I have found the answers—but because I no longer believe there are real answers in this world. Each of my searches has ended in another query. Each answer has led to another question. The thing that changed my life, started my conscious spiritual quest, and was the turning point for my life, was giving up the idea that I could find answers concerning the Divine Plan. Instead, I decided to wait for the answers to find me. I felt that if there was a Divine Source, it would reveal itself to me if I waited. The more I give up the search, the more that Divine awareness comes to me.

I do not suggest that you give up searching as long as searching for anything—a job, a companion, or even your Divine Self—appeals to you. It is the searching for something that moves us along, eventually exhausts our desires, and brings us to a state where we can fully embrace the Truth. The deep desire within us to search for something else, I believe, caused the illusory experience of our separation from the Divine. Interestingly enough, it is the thing that also brings us full circle back to Oneness. For in Oneness, our natural state, searching for anything is impossible. "Seek and you shall find" truly means seek and you shall be led to the awareness that there is nothing to seek.

How to Love Your Neighbor

To love others and our self, we must be willing to give up our concepts. It is our concept of our self and others that blinds us to the Truth. We develop self-concepts or egos to get love. These self-concepts need a great deal of defense and support, for they are always untrue and without foundation. They are simply mental pictures of who we would like to be. They define and limit us no matter whether they are labeled positive or negative. No human concept is ever sufficient to define a Divine *Being*.

We all have trouble seeing our own self-concepts. My book, *Accepting*, describes a very effective method of using what we dislike in others as the key to identifying what we dislike about ourselves. We create concepts about ourselves to cover up the portions of ourselves we dislike and think are unlovable. By releasing our perceptions and concepts about others, we free ourselves. One of the best ways to release concepts about people we dislike is to find some quality they have for which we can be truly grateful. As we keep extending this gratitude for their good qualities on a daily basis, we begin to see the truth about them. As we free them from our limited concepts of who they are, we free ourselves.

As we love and *accept* others, we always experience the same sense of freedom ourselves. The opposite is also true. As we criticize others, we condemn and jail ourselves. So the answer to the question "How do I learn to love myself?" is to first begin to love others. The more people you include in your scope of love and appreciation, the more you will begin to feel you are lovable. And who are we to love? Everyone who comes into our life. To love unconditionally, we must not choose only those who appeal to us or those who are like us. We don't have to spend our lives with difficult people, but we do have to appreciate who they are and bless them.

Often it is difficult to see something in another for which we can be grateful. For help, we can always turn to our inner guide. He and He alone sees all parties clearly. He will help us see the true loving *being* in the other person and thereby free us to see the Divine *being* within our self. This always works because of the Spiritual Law that giving and receiving are the same. Incidentally, I have found that the more difficult the other person is to love, the greater the blessings that flow when we are able to appreciate them.

Unconditional love
is a gift
of freedom
I give
myself.

CHAPTER 6

❧

The Effects of
Illusory Creation

Why Do We Create an Illusory Self?

The reason we created our "egos" is because our Real Self was not capable of being controlled in the manner we wanted. We could not individualize and get the special-ness we sought while our awareness was of Oneness. So we set about creating another being, one over which we had control. We thought this would bring us happiness. To do this, we literally created an illusory identity. We then assumed this identity.

Human beings begin this process from the moment they are born into this world. They begin making a being that they hope will bring them happiness and approval. The frustration is that no matter how hard we work to create a successful human being, it always fails in time. Through all of this, our real *being* continues unaffected and unchanged. It is interesting to note that those who love us seem to be able to see our real *being* no matter what we try to create. We cannot make or change our spiritual *being*; it was created by our Creator. We have been given the power to create, but we do not have the power to change Creation. Our attempt to change our *being* only seems to work in our dreams. Our efforts to perpetuate another existence causes us pain and stress, and these attempts ultimately fail because of their illusory nature. Thus, our soul's consciousness, our spiritual *being,* always brings us back to Reality. This is the basis of what I call the *being* process, which is always operational and requires only our awareness to be experienced.

Relationships and **Being**

In this awakening process, we do not choose to *be;* rather, we begin to recognize that *being* is happening here and now despite all our attempts to create something else. A good example is found in our relationships. Often we try to change ourselves in order to get love and approval from another. For a while, our happiness in getting love from the other covers up the effort of maintaining the type of person we think they want. We try to be a _____ . (You fill in the blank). This trying to be something requires that we temporarily control or hide what we are. We are willing to keep up this facade in order to get love and approval from the other. That person, in turn, is usually doing the same thing. This honeymoon will last only so long, since our *being* eventually cries out for expression and demands to be released from the constraints. Now the fallacy that we can compromise ourselves and succeed is revealed. The other person may withdraw their love if it was based on our false image. At this point, rather than seeing what we have done, we usually blame the other person for not appreciating us. The cycle continues as we seek for another who will match our fantasies, and we begin the sacrifice again.

Whether it is a relationship involving our work, our love life, or our spiritual path, this cycle will continue until we make peace with our real *being*. The reason it is so hard to make peace with our *being* is that it often does not match our pictures of what a successful human should be or even our pictures of what a spiritual being would be. Our *being* is not capable of manipulation. Trying to control it is like trying to control the compass on a ship so it will match our idea of the right direction, and then complaining when we get lost. It is a very important awareness to realize we need not seek to control our spiritual *being,* but rather, we need to accept it.

Being is the great secret of life and the reason we are in this earthly human experience. The process of *being* is the process of reclaiming and accepting the real you. To truly *be,* you must suspend all concepts of who you are and what you want. You must be willing to release the fantasies of who you wish you were and see the *being* you are as the perfect expression of your Divine Self. The reason parts of our past are often looked upon with compassion is that we have turned them into the fantasy of what we wanted our past to be. We do not remember what it truly was. That is fine and often necessary if we are unable to deal with the pain of what we think actually happened, but it denies the vitality and rightness of who we are. In terms of your human identity, much may have been done that was wrong both *by* you and *to* you. In Reality, you have never done anything that is really wrong, and no one has ever done anything really wrong to the real you, the Divine *Being* you are.

Making Peace with the Past

When we are willing to accept the essence of who we are, we will no longer hide our failures and exaggerate our successes. These two terms, *failure* and *success,* will become meaningless. The failures and successes, right and wrong actions, and our good and bad traits all can combine to become part of our expression. Often what we call our failures are the most important and beneficial parts of our earthly experience, from a spiritual standpoint. It is very freeing. Even more, it is a state of dominion to realize that our true *being* is operating perfectly all the time despite what we think or what others say. I can assure you that the world will never approve of or accept your spiritual *being* until you claim it for yourself. Then it won't matter.

Never underestimate how powerful our desire for worldly acceptance is and how difficult it is to follow our soul's consciousness. Several years ago, I had a most unique awakening. I went upstairs to work on my computer, and while I clearly had in mind what I wanted to record from my daily meditation, I did not get to work immediately. Several distractions occurred, and when I finally returned to the computer, it was after lunch. As I turned it on, my menu offered me both the program that contains this book, and a series of games that a friend installed for me. I punched up a game and proceeded to play it—not only for the entire afternoon, but into the early evening. I felt guilty every time I thought about getting back to work, but the game fascinated me. I became obsessed with winning. Finally, I stopped about 7:30 in the evening, having missed making myself dinner. I was very embarrassed about my loss of a day and my waste of time in such a silly and fruitless enterprise.

Then the simple question hit me: "Did I enjoy it?" The answer was yes. I also realized I had seldom ever spent a day just playing. Could I not give myself one afternoon to just play a game? Did I have to have a reason? It was hard to really accept what my soul wanted to do, since I could see no purpose in it. What is right is always defined by society. Shouldn't we take time to question it and ask our inner *being* what it wants and desires?

What is purposeful must fit into the norm of contribution to the system of existence here. Would I apply the same standard to my dreams, deciding which ones are purposeful and which are wasted? Feeling guilty, it took a while to make peace with my wasted day. Being willing to write about it helped me acknowledge my soul's direction. I am aware, on some level, that I really enjoyed a break in my routine. I am also becoming increasingly aware that I judge my activities on a scale that is set by others. In my private activity, even when I'm totally alone, there is pressure to be purposeful and productive.

I work in the yard not only because I enjoy the plants and the outdoors, but also so that I will have a socially acceptable home. It all needs to go together so I can feel good about it. Isn't this good feeling really one of knowing we will get approval from others? Could you enjoy just digging in the ground and then filling in the hole later with no purpose but to enjoy digging? Are we not slaves to the demands of society to be productive, which is really a way of conforming to a pattern? Maybe you should try to spend some time doing nothing productive just to touch the guilt that attaches to it. Social pressure keeps us trapped and covers up the yearnings of our *being*. Guilt is a constraint on our expression and a mold that keeps us from exploration and joy.

I merely point out this example as a small indication of

how we keep our *being* from speaking to us. We demand that it make sense, fit our pattern of social living, and match our concepts of what we think we are *human*, not *spiritual, beings.* I am sure that as spiritual *beings,* the concept of productivity is never considered. Instead, our *being's* expression would simply be manifesting joy and harmony. There is no standard against which we are measured since perfection cannot be measured. The wasted afternoon has been duplicated many times during the last five years, and I have often felt guilty about not working harder to finish this manuscript. It was not until now, during this final editing, that I realized I have not been ready to finish the **Being** book. The retreat needed to be sold, and I needed one year away from my mountaintop existence to be able to view the whole drama objectively.

Being *Denies Conflict*

We have no problems between us. We need no more protection from each other than our left hand needs protection from our right hand. It is natural for us to exist in harmony and joy without effort. Now the most beautiful part of this is that we are in harmony despite what we see and think is happening. In Reality, we are one *being*. Thus, our actions, even in the illusion, are always leading to love, joy, and life as an end result. We do not see this because we think we are an individual with individual needs. So I think

I have an individual will, and your will is in conflict at times with mine. That is because as an individual I only see from one point of view. Let us back up and see from the point of view of everyone concerned with the situation. If we can move back far enough, we will see harmony at work. That is why in retrospect, we often see the pattern we missed when the events were occurring. All you have to do to get clarity is to *be*. If you do this, you will realize that your *being* is naturally in harmony with everything.

Let me give you an example of how quickly our ego can enter a situation. Until recently, I have been a self-published author, as I mentioned earlier. I have enjoyed this role because it gives me lots of freedom. I am very proud of the fact that I have never tried to sell my books and yet they have grown steadily in popularity. I try to follow my guidance—not only in writing them, but also in the entire distribution process. I felt that I was free of any ego concepts concerning my books and have often stated in my lectures that I not only never set out to be an author, but that I had no problem with being led in another direction if that was my guidance.

I have several friends who also lecture and write books. One day while visiting one of my friends, he stated that he too was writing a book about inner guidance. I told him I had no problem with that since the concept was thousands of years old, and I certainly had no patent on the idea. He then told me his title, which was very similar to my **Listening** book title. He even used the term *listening,* which I felt was unique to my work. I asked him not to use that title and suggested it would lead to confusion. He said he would try to do something but seemed little concerned with the consequences. The result was the publication of his book with a very similar title. I struggled with this for several months. I could not decide what to do—whether to call his publisher and try to stop this infringement or to just let it go. I have a great deal of love for this man, and I admire his work, but all that was clouded over by a feeling of profound disappointment that he was not more aware of the effects his actions would have on my work.

I finally asked my inner guide what to do. It came as no surprise that I was told I had accepted the ego concept that I was an author and believed that my well-being was dependent on writing and lecturing. I asked for help in releasing my tight grasp on this false identity. My ego was screaming about how people looking for my book would buy the wrong one and how my income would be depleted by the promotional efforts of a large publishing company riding on the reputation my books had built over the last ten-plus years. Logically that all made sense; spiritually it was nonsense. I was told in guidance to release all my doubts and fears and give love to all concerned. I was reminded that I published my first 500 books in the hopes that it might help just one person, and never because I would make any money from my efforts. I was also reminded that the growth in *Listening's* publication over the years was not from my efforts but was part of God's plan. If God wanted another book or a hundred books about inner guidance, that was not my business. I would be cared for regardless of what happened. I was merely part of the awakening process around the world, and I was not the author or owner of any spiritual idea.

My release of the concept took time, but it is now complete. I never worried about the effect of this publication again. I am sure that the incident was forgotten and forgiven because it took me nearly a half hour to reconstruct what happened from the scribbled notes I had written several years ago about it. My friend is and has always been a most valued associate. He has helped me in numerous ways but never more than when he helped me remember that I am not any ego concept, not even a spiritual author. My true identity I share with him: *We are God's beloved children, and we are always doing God's Will surrounded by His Love.*

CHAPTER 7

Moving Beyond
Disappointment and Loss

Being *in the World*

You have probably heard that one ought to be *in* this world but not to be *of* this world. It is important to be in this world, for there is much to experience here. We are here for a purpose, and that can be simply stated as discovering that nothing can change eternal Love. We are not here to try to *escape* from the problems of the world. We are here to demonstrate their powerlessness to affect our lives. Those on a spiritual path must learn to detach from material rewards as well as human frailty and failings. You have heard me state over and over that you need to release your expectations, plans, desires, and needs. This detachment is the key to spiritual awareness, but in execution we usually do not take this act of release far enough.

As long as we are releasing the things in this world we do not like, it is an easy task. The difficulty begins as we find that our most valued concepts, such as truth, loyalty, and love do not work and need to be released—when applied on a human level. Let me emphasize this point, which seems simple but often is missed. All human qualities, whether good or bad, are not worthy of you; they will not bring you satisfaction, and they will eventually fail. Disappointment and a sense of loss should be signals to us that we are holding on to material values. Disappointment could not exist unless there was first some expectation. Expectation is the sign of conditional thinking. This thinking states that if I do this or that, I can expect this or that result. The spiritual point of view has no expectation. Whatever is given spiritually must be given freely, with no conditions.

You may have started this journey of following inner guidance in the hopes that it would make the world a better place in which to live. You may, through inner guidance, hope to find your proper job, your soulmate, or just help others. As we grow spiritually, we often find our best plans failing; usually it happens when we are ready to be free of the things of this world. For example, we are loving and forgiving, and the other person does not respond and maybe even attacks us. We find our perfect job, partner, or place to live through being guided, and in the end it changes. At this point when your best efforts fail, it is easy to feel frustrated, even betrayed. Sometimes this disappointment and loss seems to have been caused by our friends and even desertion by God.

Facing the Pain of Injustice

I am sure this is what Jesus went through in the garden of Gethsemene as he awaited betrayal by friends, desertion and denial by his spiritual family, and crucifixion by his enemies. We all come to this place where, despite our best, most loving actions, the world does not respond in a loving way. This is not a time for sadness. This happens because we are ready to loosen our attachment to the material world. We are ready to free the world from our demand that it conform to our ideas. We are ready to release the idea that this human experience will give us anything. I know from personal experience that this disappointment feels like falling into a black hole. Yet each time we face it and move through it, there is always a great awareness of freedom. We must make peace with the fact that the spiritual path of awakening is not a series of lessons in how to make this world work better. It is release from this world's limitations. This world does not work, and not even God's Will can make it work because it is an illusion. Illusions do not work—that's the good news. They are not bad or evil, nor do they need to be changed, fixed, or overcome by love. The truth is, "Illusions are not real and simply do not work." Therefore, they fail of their own accord. Do not look for justice in this world, for there is none. However, neither is there injustice. The world is a neutral place.

The Justice Trap

One of my biggest issues has been my search for justice. I used to pride myself on my fairness and responsibility. Like all the world's illusory concepts, my desire for justice worked for a while. It began to crack early when, as a young law student, I served in the Army's legal department. All my efforts to bring justice to the cases I worked on failed. I remember one soldier who went AWOL (absent without leave) several times. His wife kept getting into trouble as a result of not having enough money and, of course, each time he was AWOL, his wife's allotment was canceled. Every time I got his records straight and restored his allotment, he would go AWOL again. After three tries, I realized that nothing I could do would change the Army's reaction or his desire to run off and avoid problems.

In business, I have tried to be fair and give employees an interest only to have them leave and start up a competitive business on the money I had to pay them to get my ownership back. I've been stuck with a large loan on which I was a co-signor as a favor to friends. I've been stolen blind by a manager of my restaurant who begged me for a job and said he would never forget my saving his career.

These types of experiences have occurred often with people I trusted and treated fairly. My search for justice has only been useful in bringing me to the place where I can release my search. Actually, it is not a release. I have simply outgrown these concepts. If this book signifies a deep theme in my life, it has been the release of my need for the world to be just and fair.

We cannot call unwanted events unfair and unjust and thereby make them wrong. Don't mistake what I say. Injustice covers everything from disappointment and annoyance to thoughts of vengeance and retribution. If you have the slightest feeling of discomfort about any outcome that has happened to you and you are searching for the guilty person, that means you are holding another responsible for making your desired outcome occur. A fair and just outcome is nothing more than having things turn out as you think they should. There is no standard of justice in this world except the one you are demanding. What is just for one person is not always just for another. Only in Heaven is there justice, and that exists because it is unconditional Love, not justice.

Justice Is a Non-Issue

Justice is not something to seek, nor is injustice something to avoid. No one can be unjustly treated on the spiritual level, the only real experience. No one has the power to change God's plan. That plan is going on all the time. The form changes, but the plan is always that you will awaken to remember who you are. Our human plan is to make the world more comfortable and avoid awakening. When our experiences match our desires and plans, we feel justice has been done. We may even pretend that our plan is God's plan. Not true. God's plan is that there is no illusory world.

The blessing of injustice is that we learn that there is nothing here that will ever make us happy or give us peace. *Nothing* taken away from us even when we think it is important is still *nothing*. When we release the world from the need to participate in our plans and concepts, the result is miraculous. Now the world reflects God's Will and our Divine Will since we are not forcing our human will upon it. When we stop interfering with God's Creation by projecting our false creation upon it in the name of justice, nothing is left but perfection. We are the creators of these illusions even when they have wonderful names, such as *justice*. No matter the fancy or venerable names, their only effect is to cloud our recognition of Reality. Most of the world's current teaching has as its purpose the creation of better illusions, not the removal of illusions. These efforts have no effect on Reality. I merely point it out so you will not be surprised when your efforts to create more positive, just, or harmonious illusions fail you.

Perfect Justice Now

In a state of *being,* we see how perfect every person is in our life. We see how they are assisting us in the realization of our spiritual nature and our perfection. In short, we simply see what was always there. Justice and fairness are not our responsibility. In fact, we must realize that we cannot know, much less bring about, what would be fair for all concerned. So the way to peace is for us to give up all attempts to bring about justice. Here's a little story told to me by my inner guide that illustrates the justice of God's plan. It was the answer to a question I have had most of my life.

The Prodigal Son... A Creation Story

Bottom line, my question is, "If God made everything perfect and good, where did it all go wrong?" Even if what's wrong is an illusion, how is an illusion possible, and why does God allow it to continue? Why does God allow injustice?

In answer to this puzzle, I've been told by my inner guide that the Prodigal Son story is a good explanation of what happened in Creation and why nothing is really wrong. This story from the Bible is about a rich man who had two sons. They worked on their father's farm and lived a wonderful life. One day the youngest son decided to leave and seek his fortune on his own. So he asked his father for his inheritance, left the farm, and went to the city. The bright lights were too much for him, and soon the youngest son had spent his fortune foolishly. To survive, he took a job tending pigs and had to live in the pig sty because he had no money. He wanted to go home, but he was afraid to face his father. Finally, in desperation, he returned home planning to be a field hand for his father since that was better than the pig sty. The son was sure his father would never forgive him, but he hoped his father might take pity on him.

When his father saw him coming home, he ran to meet his son and wept with joy. He washed him and put him in new clothes and held a great feast in celebration of his return. Meanwhile, the older brother heard about this and was very angry. He said to his father, "I have worked hard and not wasted my inheritance, and yet you never gave me all this attention." The father tells the older son not to worry because "you have always been with me."

∽ ∽ ∽

I've read this story many times, and frankly I've always thought that the father was being unfair to the older son who was frugal and hardworking. My inner guide asked me at the end of the story, "Why was the father celebrating? What had the younger son learned?" I then knew the answer. The younger son knew where he wanted to be, and he made a decision to be home with his father at any price. I also saw that the older son did not know the value of what he had because he was jealous of his younger bother although he had not faced the misery his brother had endured. He had been able to stay home and enjoy the good life all the time. Without the experience of living somewhere else, the younger son might never have known the value of being with his father. It was not something the father could give the son. The father probably knew what would happen if his son left, but like all good fathers, he trusted his son to make the right decision in the end and waited for his return. Is leaving home a vital part of the son's education? Is that why we go through this earthly illusion? To decide where we really want to be?

Yes, we are created perfect, and since we are given free will, we are not required to stay in Reality (paradise). Given the ability to choose, we must make our own decisions. These decisions can include not experiencing Oneness. This choice could not occur in Reality, but it could be experienced in a state of illusion. It may be necessary for us to leave Paradise in order to appreciate who we really are and make the decision where we want to be.

While this world of duality (good and evil) may be merely an illusion, it is a very convincing illusion. From our experiences here, we will eventually decide not to stay. By deciding to return home, we make the only decision that will make us happy. Thus, this experience allows the son to make the perfect choice, the one choice that will bring him real happiness. The son completes the part of growing up that the father could not complete; he decides of his own free will to love and be with his father. There is no mistake, no punishment, and no guilt. All is as it was meant to be.

Thus, the issue of justice becomes irrelevant since the experience of being away from home and the desire to return home is all that matters. Whether justice or injustice brings this about, the outcome is the same. Were both sons treated fairly? Yes, they were both cared for and loved by their father. They were both given the freedom to do as they wished. We don't know—maybe the older son will need the experience of leaving home, also. If he does, I am sure his father will be waiting.

CHAPTER 8

The Essence of Your *Being*

A New Insight into Guidance

Sometimes my *being* takes the form of an inner voice, and sometimes it is just a feeling about things. It can feel like either an attraction or a repellent. Sometimes it takes the form of desire that I cannot rationalize, such as my deep need to live near the water. Sometimes it takes on an identity that speaks aloud to me or that dialogues with me. Sometimes it takes the form of who I really am at my deepest level. Another word that might better define this last manifestation is my *essence*. This is something I am, beyond what I try to be. In some cases, my essence has gotten me into trouble, and sometimes it leads me to my greatest achievements. As I am more aware of this essence, I realize that it is the part of me I like most, regardless of what others think. It is the part I'm most unwilling to change. When I compromise this core me, or essence, I am never happy. My essence is so basic to who I am that I return to it the moment I stop trying to be something else.

Let me describe mine and how it manifests so you may be able to see your essence more clearly. I am certain that our essence or *being* is the basic spirit of each of us. It's what makes you and me capable of our present individual manifestations. It may be what we sought to express more fully when we tried to separate from our Source. The interesting part is that when we use it to separate from others, it brings us pain and loneliness. When we accept it in ourselves and others, we find connection, love, and joy. We'll discuss this further in a moment, but first let's identify what this essence is. It may surprise you.

Essence and Being

In my case, my *being* might be described as a questioner, a doubter, and a person with great need to know how things work. It is not an intellectual curiosity, although I would prefer that it was. It is a practical need to find out how things really work so I can use them. My essence has lots of ideas. It loves adventure and wants to explore everything. It also loves to play. It loses interest when the search becomes too complicated unless this search takes the form of a challenge. It wants to participate in the action rather than observe it. It does not place great value on learning from others. It wants to find its own unique solutions. When things are going too smoothly, my essence often creates an internal struggle just to shake things up. This can lead me to make choices that result in my feeling alone and separate. My spirit manifests as one who wants to experience its own truth, not the truth of another.

I have many times longed to be able to join the group and feel comforted by its support. Always something in me feels compromised by going along with the crowd. In college, when most professors and students were Democrats, I was a Republican. Then when more people became Republicans in the early 1980s, I felt compelled to switch to the Democratic party. This contrary part of my individuality caused me to turn down a scholarship to a prestigious law school, which I did not feel I had earned on merit. It has caused me to end several comfortable relationships that I felt were not providing all that I hoped was possible. It has caused me to stay in projects when most reasonable people abandoned them. The result has been that I have often been left alone to carry a burden I really did not want. To most people, these negative manifestations of my *being* would be viewed as fatal flaws. Many times that has been the result, yet this same essence led me to demand a direct relationship with God, and that decision has changed my life and set me on a path that is unbelievably satisfying.

At present, I am making peace with my essence and all its manifestations as my *being*. Its expression is far more complicated than this brief description. I am sure I do not see all of it, nor do I understand its full impact. I am learning to recognize it and love it, not just the part I like, but also the parts of my essence that cause me to feel alone and separate. Thus, an important part of *being* is not only seeing our oneness and connection with others, but also to use *being* to bring all parts of ourselves into an integrated whole that we can appreciate and love.

Changing Our Essence

I do not believe that this essence we each have is something we can modify. I do believe we can misuse it and, therefore, we can also learn to use it properly. What is necessary is to appreciate our own wonderful manifestation and also to appreciate and support others in expressing their essence. It may be difficult to support others when their essence seems in conflict with our own. We cannot do this using human judgement, but only if we viewed these other people as spiritual manifestations. As we begin to see how our essence is constantly leading us back to union with the Divine Will, we begin to see how others are on the same journey even when they have taken different paths. Re-*union* with our Divine Source is all that is truly important on earth, and it is all that is ever really happening here.

It is interesting that our essence appears both in what we would call spiritual guidance and the guidance we get from our ego or worldly mind. While this essence may not always make us successful or well liked in this world, I am convinced that awareness of it is the most direct path to our spiritual reunion. When viewed from this standpoint, we can get a more accurate picture—not only of what we are about—but how others are following their paths. As we begin to love our *being* and other *beings* in all their manifestations, we can release our tight grip on trying to control situations. At our present state of awareness, we seem to be separate *beings,* but we are all connected. The more I am aware of my *being,* the more I feel connected with everything. The more I can love my essence and get to know it, the more I can see your essence and appreciate its impact on your spiritual awareness as well as mine.

This Essence Can Be Seen

I had the wonderful experience a few years ago of physically seeing this essence. I was waiting near a promenade along the San Diego Bay for my son to arrive and join me on a sailboat trip. People were walking along in this beautiful scene, and I was sitting on a bench and enjoying watching them. Suddenly, I became aware of a spirit inhabiting each person. I could see a different spirit in each body. The body's age, shape, and condition simply reflected the viewpoints of each individual spirit. It was as if the spirit wondered how it would feel to take on a particular form, so it had created that form and was now manifesting through it. The experience would be similar to seeing the puppeteers formerly hidden behind a curtain suddenly revealed as the source of movement for the puppets. I could no longer take the form of the body seriously. I saw each different body or puppet playing a part for a specific reason. None was better than any other.

If a beautiful girl in shorts ran by, I felt the inhabiting spirit saying that this is how it feels to be a beautiful person and have everyone look at me. If a muscular jogger ran by, I felt the spirit say that this is how it feels to be very strong and very secure in your physical ability. If an old lady with a dog ambled by, I could feel the spirit say that this is how it is to be old, totally alone, and pour out all your affection on a cute little dog. If a mature couple strolled by hand in hand, I could feel the spirit say that this is how it is to have many years together and know each other so well that words were unnecessary. Each individual carried an emotional message for me. Each represented a personification of how life felt in that particular individual manifestation. I felt so much love for each person's essence. I saw that each was unique and beautiful and part of the dramatic interplay. Each color, each shape, and each personification was special and wonderful.

Why Essence Takes Form

Let's examine why our essence is experiencing this life. I believe we come into this existence with a personality. This personality or essence comes with a desire for, and a plan to have, various experiences. No two personalities are alike. Even though they may share the same experience, the effect is different on every essence involved. As this essence expresses itself through various cycles of life, from babyhood to old age it is changed and shaped. The experiences impact the essence or spirit in various ways, but the final outcome is a realization by the essence of its real desires. As we discussed in the Prodigal Son myth, the basis of the experience was for the son to decide on his own where he wanted to be. This is what I feel our essence is doing. While the basic nature of the essence changes very little, the manifestation of our essence is greatly changed by these experiences.

We can see our essence at an early age. My mother reported that even as a small child I needed to know how things worked. I could take no one's word for what happened. This included putting my hand in a fire to feel how hot it was despite her warning that I would burn myself. I am very grateful that she did not stop me from having that experience. I dissected nearly every mechanical device I could find, from clocks and fishing reels to cars and boats. In my mid-teens, I built a crude cottage by the lake and lived in it for a short time. I later traded this cottage for a moldy trailer in our front yard. At ten, I built a boat to explore our lake. It looked strangely like a coffin. My mother was sure it was. At 14, I built a small race boat so I could explore faster. It, too, was of doubtful seaworthiness, but it was mine. All this was very important to me despite the fact that our family had two very stable boats that I was welcome to use any time.

This do-it-yourself approach has continued to play out in various aspects throughout my life. Most of these experiences would be judged less than satisfactory by anyone with reasonable quality-control standards. Yet something in me desires to personally explore and experience. I am slowly making my peace with my perverse essence. I am allowing it to manifest more easily, and I no longer judge the results of its efforts so harshly. I hate to take lessons, go to meetings, join groups, or be told what to do even when I know it is for my benefit. I'd rather take the longer, slower, more difficult path of doing it by myself. I avoid the more rational approach of learning from others' mistakes. Why? Just because that's how I am. That's my essence.

Accepting Our Essence

Being is making peace or, even better, *accepting* our essence. We need to give up the idea that successful spiritual growth is measured by how much we can adapt our essence to a conventional form. In a nutshell, our spiritual essence is not always nice, but it is always you. You are a spiritual individualization here and now, and you are in the process of gaining full awareness of what that is. Full manifestation of your individuality and complete expression of your essence does eventually lead to Reality. This road, however, is narrow and difficult because there are few guideposts and no maps of how to do it, since every path is unique. Love of yourself as you are and love of the essence of all others is total unconditional Love. Unconditional Love is the best guideline and can be followed by *listening* to your inner being.

We need to get in touch with our own spiritual *being* and let it speak to us. At the outset, it may feel as if it contains some of our worst flaws. It is not our job to change what we call our flaws. As we continue to trust our deepest feelings, the process reveals itself. Our *being* creates a series of experiences that will reveal to us our true identity. If we seek to suppress our essence, we delay the path to our awareness. Our job is not to change ourselves, but to express and *accept* ourselves and others.

The Divine Plan will naturally sort out what is valuable from what is not. Our job is merely to be conscious of its effects on our manifestation. This is a vital point and is very different from many approaches that stress various forms of self-control and improvement. We cannot improve ourselves. Any changes we make are merely changes of form. It is the Divine Source that effects real change. Our job is simply to be aware of our faulty thinking as we see it and offer it up for correction. When you clearly see the damaging effects of any faulty belief in your life, in that moment you no longer want it. It is then that God instantly removes the belief and its effects. This is the only true form of healing, physical or otherwise; all else is mental mind control, which can shift the manifestation of the belief but does nothing to change the actual belief. Unchanged, the belief manifests in a new way but with similar limiting results.

Measuring Success

Problems occur when we try to measure our progress in terms of spiritual awareness. We may find that the expression of our *being* does not bring us immediate love and approval. Seldom will the expression of your spiritual essence bring you worldly rewards. That is because spiritual manifestation is very threatening to the worldly thought structure. Most people "love" those who do things in a way they approve. The group withholds "love" (approval) when individuals do not act in ways that the majority calls normal or proper. Since no two essences are exactly alike, at some point the full expression of each individual essence will create conflict and differences within the group. Unless we can love beyond the differences and see the value of each *being's* full expression, we will reject the person creating conflict and seek the company of another, more compatible person. Of course, that will also fail at the point when they more fully express their essence.

The only measurement of our spiritual success that is valid is a positive answer to the question, "Does this feel true or right to me?" This question needs to be continually asked and answered. There is no permanent answer since the process is one of evolution. What felt right to you yesterday may not feel true to you today. You can easily see the fallacy of asking the group or others what you feel is right. If this question is not asked and the individual seeks to ignore his or her deep inner feelings, the results appear in other ways. The stress and frustration of trying to suppress our essence can manifest in physical pain—that is, headaches and sleeplessness, illness, and in restrictions of the body's functions. Many of our current social problems are the manifestation on a large scale of the refusal on everyone's part to support each person's expression of their unique spiritual *being*.

The fear may be voiced that the uncontrolled expression of each individual essence would bring chaos and social disorder. That is not true, but the opposite is. If we do not support such expression, the result is social disorder. While the individual essence is different for each of us, at this human level of existence there is an overall harmony that results when *beings* seek their full expression. That is because the Divine Source of each individual *being* is not in conflict; it is the same. Strange as it sounds, our essence comes from One Source, and what we call individual is actually One *Being*. What the world seeks is harmony and peace. This can be attained by expression, but not by suppression. It is attained naturally when each of us recognizes the beauty of others and supports their expression of their spiritual essence.

The measure, then, of our success is a continual positive response to such questions as, "Do I feel like my true self? Do I support others in being their real self and fulfilling their desires? Do I do this without compromise of my own essence?" Despite the worldly fears that such techniques are not practical, my experience to date in using these systems is just the opposite. When everyone fully expresses themselves and when such expression is honored, the results are very positive even in terms of material success.

The Oneness of Everything

This Oneness concept can be expanded not only to every person, but to every thing on the planet. We need to recognize the essence of each thing and allow it to unfold. In a world that is shrinking through rapid and expanded communication, the necessity of supporting the emergence of individual expression in each person, group, and organization becomes even more vital. We need to go beyond the narrow desire to control what is different and not force others to adopt our beliefs. For example, democracy as practiced in the United States is a great idea, but it cannot be exported in our particular form to others who have a different belief system. Our concept of freedom can be shared with all. Freedom does not seek to force another to act in a particular way. Thus, we can support freedom and equality, but we enter dangerous ground, which only brings us increased conflict when we define how these concepts will manifest.

I am most excited about the future. While I do not think the year 2000 will bring any special blessings, I do see great changes occurring as we become more aware of our interconnectedness and our need for individualization. These two concepts are not in conflict, but rather, are essential to each other. One given prominence over the other results in tyranny or chaos. A natural process is slowly occurring in which we can be seen as individual and as part of all others, two sides of one basic system that is interdependent and individual.

Our worldly experience often makes it impossible to understand how individual *beings* can possibly be singular in nature and yet joined as One. As with all spiritual truths, the Oneness of *being* cannot be explained, but it can be experienced here and now. Think for a moment of the connection made when someone supports your spirit's expression. Nothing is so appreciated as *acceptance* of one's self just as it manifests. This *acceptance* expresses as love between all involved. *Acceptance* of our selves makes us want to support others in their expression of their individuality. There is one thing everyone wants, all who have been here, are here now, or will come to this world. That secret longing is a desire to be loved and appreciated. Love can only be satisfying if it is based on *acceptance* of a person's essence. This *acceptance* joins us together even on the worldly plane and creates a feeling of understanding and oneness.

CHAPTER 9

The State of Changeless Joy

The Need to Change

To experience Reality in our present state, we need to release the need to change things—even ourselves. We can also begin to experience Reality as we release the concept that we can make real choices within the illusion. The only real choice in the dualistic experience is the choice to release the idea of others and experience Oneness. This one choice goes beyond merely changing our thought processes. It is the willingness to actually experience no others. We cannot experience this Oneness or make real choices without the assistance of inner guidance. Thus, our *being* is the only source we have that offers real choices.

As we begin to become aware of Reality, we begin to

see the falsity of judging between good and bad, justice and injustice, love and hate, or pain and pleasure. We begin to awaken to the truth that these concepts are merely a matter of our personal judgment. What is good to one may be bad to another. What is just to one person can be unjust to another. What is love in one moment is hate a few moments later. We can begin to realize that our human perception is flawed. Until we see this flaw, we will continue to defend what we call our judgment. This defense traps us in the duality illusion. When we find another wrong and attack him or her, rather than question our judgment, we become blind. In the dualistic world, judgment is always inadequate because it is based on personal preference rather than Truth.

Giving Up the Desire to Judge

We can at least suspend our desire to judge even if we find it difficult to give it up entirely. We can make the one choice that leads to peace and joy by letting our inner guide choose for us. Having given our *being* the opportunity to see for us, we can then act on this perfect judgment. Sounds simple, doesn't it, but the application is often tricky and difficult. The farther along the path we go following inner guidance, the more that following our inner guide comes in conflict with our sacred beliefs. That is why it is so important to retain an attitude of *accepting* everything. As we release more and more to our inner guide's judgment, we are not so much directed to take specific actions as we are given new insights and a clearer perspective. Rather than being given something to do about the problem, we are usually given a new way to view the situation, which often makes action unnecessary. If there is action required, it is usually easy, direct, and simple. Often we see that the problem is no problem when we turn to inner guidance.

The Difference Between Pleasure and Joy

One of the hurdles I have found difficult to cross is the confusion between pleasure and joy. Joy, as I am using the term, is a spiritual state flowing naturally from Reality. This joy never changes, never diminishes, and never increases. It is a constant state. It is not measured by the amount of pleasure we feel, nor is it diminished by the amount of turmoil we experience. Pleasure and pain are part of the dualistic world. They are often simply measurements of how well our dreams and aspirations are being fulfilled. If we are with those we love, and they are acting in the way we desire, we feel great pleasure. If they do not act in the desired way, we may feel great pain. If they are not physically close, we are often in agony. None of this has anything to do with spiritual joy. In fact, when we properly understand spiritual joy, we can experience it no matter what we feel on a human level. The converse is also true. In our present state, we can feel pain and still experience our spiritual joy. We should not measure our joy in terms of our human pleasure. Joy and pleasure represent two different worlds—the first is real and the other is imaginary and subject to constant change.

I think this realization became most clear when I dealt with the end of relationships. At times, there has been an underlying sadness that remained with me for several years even when I did not want the relationship to continue. When I feel sad, I do not try to get rid of or deny my hurt and disappointment. I simply turn to my inner *being* and ask for solace. Healing requires that we acknowledge how we really feel and not pretend. Trying to change our feelings, to hide them, or deny them, not only doesn't work but it intensifies the pain and places the healing on a level where our inner guidance cannot reach it. Our job is not to fix ourselves but to become aware of our false concepts and to offer them up for correction. If I look at my pain clearly, I usually see that it is based upon my plans for my life. When I release this sadness and my plans to my inner guide, who is the only source of joy for me, I get a clear picture of how my desires limit me. In time, I will always see how the Divine Plan enriches me.

I have learned that my sadness and grief were not as much a result of what happened, but actually represented my grief over my lost fantasies. My pleasure is based on getting what I want, and my pain is caused by the loss of what I think I needed. These are not real needs, but my needs as I defined them. I can feel either pleasure or pain depending on how well I decided my fantasies are met. I also have another choice—a real choice. I can feel love for others and desire that they find what is best for them regardless of whether it matches my plans. As I let go of my plans for myself and others, I can see what is really happening, and this brings me spiritual joy. It is most interesting that despite this period of sadness, each new relationship has been more fulfilling than the previous one. I have experienced this increased joy in all my relationships—not only with women, but with my work, my friends, and places where I live. I have to honestly say that it is strange that I ever grieve, since something better always comes along.

Joy Is Not Conditional

I can see that my real joy is not dependent on events or others. I do not need to change the events so they meet my perceived needs. Rather, my perceived needs and desires need to be changed based on what is happening. My *being* is bringing me all I truly need. This may or may not match my plans and desires. My desires are related to my view of who I am, and at this level, that is a very limited concept. My needs and desires are constantly changing and always will be changing. All these concepts are based on my personal viewpoint and not the universal viewpoint. There is no true joy in individual joy. Human pleasure seldom, if ever, includes everyone. Pleasure is usually specifically designated by and for one person. It may include other people, but it usually requires them to act in preplanned ways. Not being part of Oneness, this concept of pleasure will always fail to bring joy to anyone, because it is designed to bring pleasure to only one.

Jesus said to Pontius Pilate on the eve of his crucifixion, "Thou wouldst have no power over me were it not given you from above." These words have come to me often during difficult periods. Slowly, it has begun to dawn on me what Jesus meant by that statement and how it applies to everyone. No person in this world has power to harm us unless we give it to them. They cannot hurt us or make us sad or cause us pain unless we give them that power. We set ourselves up by expecting something from them. That is our ultimate reality; we literally give our joy away by placing it in the hands of another person.

When Jesus would not answer the questions put to him, his judge, Pilate, said, "Don't you know I have the power to execute you?" Jesus's reply was simply, "You do not have that power, because it resides with God, my Father." Our *being* provides us with all we need because it is our connection with our Divine Source; thus, no person has the power to withhold anything from us. The one power, the only power that can affect us, is God, Love. If we maintain our dependence on the Divine to provide what we need, regardless of the worldly event—even a crucifixion by our enemies and desertion by our friends—we can retain our spiritual joy and rise above the world of pleasure and pain. We can, through our reliance on the Divine Source, experience only this joy. The only thing that can affect that joy is if we give the power to provide our happiness and joy to other people. If we do, then we are vulnerable if they do not act as we desire them to act.

Thus, Jesus was able to walk through an experience that was seen by the world as filled with great pain and loss. All that the world considers to be important was taken from him—loyalty, friendship, fairness, justice, and even his human life. From this experience in which he was able to release all the world had to offer—friendship, justice, and human life—he emerged in his true spiritual form and demonstrated his union with Divine Love. He knew he could lose nothing of value and that nothing in the world had the power to change his true Being.

Resurrection Is Natural

On some level, resurrection is always what is happening in our lives. We are releasing our limited concepts of love and letting them be replaced with expanded concepts of Divine Love. Each seeming failure of our plans brings us closer to the Truth. Often it is the pain and not the pleasure that teaches, releases, and benefits us most. These times of loss—loss of our fantasies and dreams—are usually moments of great growth. Yet, we seek to avoid them rather than embrace them and become more aware. We waste time in senseless grief and lamentation. How much we miss the mark when we celebrate our successes in attaining human goals and mourn our failures on the altar of self-pity. As we grow in spiritual awareness, the line between success and failure becomes more blurred. We find it harder and harder to measure. We begin to question what was unquestionable at an earlier time. Our concepts of love, fairness, justice, and even the concept that we know what we need become less useful. You may find it tempting to think you are sliding backwards during these dark times, but I can assure you that despite the outward appearance, what is really happening is the birth and growth of your true *being*.

As these failures happen, we may also feel we are being asked by the Divine to give up what we value most. This is only true on a human level. On the Spiritual level, the only level that is Real, we are awakening. What no longer is worthy of or useful to us is being removed. The more deeply held the belief that we are human, the more pain we experience when our human concepts are redefined for us. The ultimate result of this loss of our concepts is always a freer, more joyful *being,* but the process seldom feels pleasurable when our perceived needs are threatened or denied. The only real answer, of course, is that we are not human, but spiritual, *beings,* and so our real joy can only come from our Divine Source. This joy is unconditional and can never be lost.

Being *Includes Abundant Supply*

The concept of *being* affirms that we always have all that we need, and whatever we need will be supplied. More supply is never a need. We merely need to open to what is being sent to us and not judge its value. So many times in the past 20 years I thought I needed something and felt that it was being withheld from me only to find out later that I had all I really needed. The story of finding my current home is a perfect illustration. As I related earlier, I was not able to buy this house when I first found it, and I felt something very important was being withheld from me. Six months later when I thought the house was sold to someone else, I found it was still available, and the timing for my ownership was far better. I know this happened because I was willing to let God provide my proper place, and rather than grieve over my loss, I relied on Divine Supply to provide me with what I needed. It might be a home, or it might be something else.

Many people have difficulty with the idea of following God's Will because they see it as requiring a sacrifice of their own will, as we mentioned earlier. This is true only if we are using our will to protect and provide for us. God's Will is that we have all that we need. When I do not have enough energy, time, or money to do a project, I must realize that nothing is wrong, and if I am to do the project, all that I need will be provided. Now supply becomes a part of my guidance.

Prayer Is Realization of the Truth

Much of what we call prayer is our petition that God make our human wishes come true. We plead for Him to lend us His power to help accomplish our human desires. It is like praying that the laws of gravity will not operate if we jump off a cliff. This is not real prayer, nor does it affect the Divine in any way. Real prayer is the desire to be aware of what truly is, not to get one's own way or to change anything. All Divine Action benefits everyone in equal amounts. It realizes that we are all part of the whole, and it is impossible that one win while another lose. Real prayer realizes that all is created good and that all is well despite the human appearances. Any prayer to change anything or to produce an outcome that we hope to be especially beneficial to us is praying amiss. We do not know what is beneficial either for others or for ourselves. I do not doubt that many think otherwise, but any prayer except to be aware of the correctness of Divine Creation is not effective because it is based on a false premise.

God's Will Works Now

Amazingly, what we see as God's power, and what is called God's Will, operates in the illusion. While it may take time, the outcome is always, ALWAYS, harmony. Hate, no matter how strong, can never last and is always replaced with love. We see throughout human history the temporary victory of hate and fear, but we also see the eventual outcome being more love and more understanding. As humans, we have a very limited view of this, and we think in terms of what is happening at this time or this moment to those I know and care about. However, with a larger perspective, we can see that the final triumph is always Truth. We can rest in peace and *be*, knowing that the final results will be love. We can realize that all that is really happening amid the death, pain, sickness, and confusion in the illusion is our awakening to Reality.

Being *Replaces Judgment*

The basic direction of all my struggle has been to bring me to a loving and peaceful place—not peaceful as the world knows it, not lack of conflict, and not rosy outcomes, but peaceful in terms of certainty and joy. A peaceful knowing that I, as part of all Creation, am well. What is happening around me and to me is merely the dispelling of illusion. The process may be noisy, fear filled, and chaotic in my limited view, but it is always the process of replacing illusion with Truth. Illusion does not die quietly, for we are all holding on to it tightly. I can kick and scream during the struggle, but it changes nothing. Why is it so hard? Think for a moment about how much effort you expend to protect your concept of who you are.

At first, I could see harmony in what happened only after a long period of time. When I was given the *listening* process, I was told, "Always ask what to do and then do it, and you will begin to see peace and harmony emerge in you life." As I did that, I was amazed by how things began to work out. However, there were times when what happened seemed unfair. When I sought to avoid or change the situation on my own, I created an internal conflict. I am never told how to change others by my inner guide. My own efforts to change others often fails, except on a temporary basis.

Continuing with the story of buying my current home, one interesting factor was that the seller was a public institution. The person responsible for the negotiation of the sale seemed to be very rigid and fearful. My judgment was that he was more interested in protecting his job than selling the house since it had been on the market for several years. During my first negotiations, I found him to be extremely difficult and inflexible. When my first escrow failed, it was hard not to feel that it was due in a large part to his personality faults. As it turned out, his cautious personality trait was a major factor in my getting the property.

What I originally saw as negative qualities turned out to be the very things that saved the property for me. It is interesting that the second escrow went through in record time, with no delay on this man's part. Once again, I had to admit that I did not know what was happening and that my judgment was meaningless. However, if you think your judgment is right and you are not willing to change it, then you will get the negative results you expect. It is only as we release our judgment that the Divine can work to change the situation.

Finally, as a result of many experiences—some of which I have related to you—I have come to the stage of welcoming *being*. Now I am told that there is little to do, little to think about, and nothing to change, not even me. I am merely to *be,* and if I am to do anything, it will open before me. Now I *listen,* mostly to be told how to connect with everything. I *listen* to the me that truly is, not to some guide apart from me. Now I am told that there is no separation between me in a physical form and my spiritual *being*. I am my Father's Son. I am a spiritual creation, no matter the present form.

*Be still
and you will
know.*

CHAPTER 10

Following God's Will

Opposing Wills Are Impossible

The foundation of *being* is living in harmony with God's Will. However, the term *God's Will* is often misunderstood because it brings up images of authority. We may think of God as a parent directing a wayward child. In most cases, we view God's Will as different from our own and a restriction on our individual expression and happiness. Nothing could be further from the Truth.

God's Will is not a power. In Reality, there are no opposing forces. In God's Creation, force is not even possible. There is only a harmony of order and love. Since all is connected and everything is interrelated, there can be opposing force. It is as impossible for the concept of *other* to exist in Reality, just as it is impossible that any part of you is opposed to you. It's not possible that your feet want one thing, your hands another, and your mind another. You don't use your mind to force all your parts to agree. There is only one mind, so every part works in harmony. Every appendage is part of you, just as all Creation is made up of God. Integration and cooperation are natural. It is impossible that one part of Creation exists in even slight disagreement. Harmony is the natural and only condition in Reality. This natural harmony is God's Will.

Since duality can only exist in illusion, so the concept of power can only exist in a delusional state. God's Will operates like a principle, rather than a power. It would be silly to talk of the power of mathematics. The principle of mathematics is the only workable way to solve numerical problems. So God's Will is the only right way to live. This Divine principle is always in operation, whether it is recognized or not, and it always operates in the same way. It creates harmony throughout all Creation. In our present state of pretending to not *be*, we have created an illusion of conflicting forces and opposing wills. Just as a mistake does not change the principle of mathematics, our illusions of conflict have no effect on Divine Laws. The mistake only affects each person's experience for as long as he or she continues to make the mistake.

Our will only seems to be capable of opposing God's Will. We seem to be living in a world with individual wills that are not in harmony. The illusion of various wills creates the illusion of chaos, which results from choosing an unconnected existence. Separate persons with separate wills would have to be at cross-purposes. In Reality this is impossible, and even in our present experience, it only appears possible until we see what is really happening. All that is ever going on both on Heaven and on Earth is a maximal exchange of love. When we do not recognize the unconditional nature of Love and its spiritual effect on our lives, we wrongly judge what is happening.

We follow God's Will by desiring to see harmony and connectedness in all creation. We seek to experience Reality when we drop the idea of our special and separate needs. This usually happens after we have exhausted all efforts to find peace, love, and harmony by using our separated will. Only then are we willing to align our will with God's Will. By releasing our separated will, we recognize what is Real and has always been. It is important to note that we can only experience what is Real—Love, Truth, and Life—when we want that experience. God's Will is never forced upon us. God's Will, Divine Love, is always there, and only your desire to see harmony is necessary for it to fill your consciousness.

We Cannot Avoid Reality

If we seek to solve mathematical problems but refuse to use the principle that 1 plus 1 are 2, we create a mistake.

If our own system states that 1 plus 1 are 3, we will at some point become frustrated when the answers don't work. The system of mathematics does not punish us for creating a different system, nor is the law of mathematics affected by our efforts to use another system. There is only one system that will bring correct answers. If we want correct results, we must join our efforts in harmony with the laws that work.

God's Will, or Laws, operate in the same way, and they govern creation. They always operate and do so equally throughout all Creation. They always assure peace, love, and harmony. When these Laws are not recognized, the results can only be loss of peace, love, and harmony. Reality's principles must be followed to get harmonious results. We cannot, for example, give less than unconditional love and hope to experience love in return. Love's principle that giving and receiving are the same is always in operation whether we recognize it or not. If we do not give love unconditionally, we do not get love; there is no other possibility.

There is, however, more to God's Will than just the operation of principle. For God's Will is Love and reflects total Love. We have chosen to individualize, but it was impossible that we could separate from Love. The Love of the Creator for the Created is without limits. Even in our dreams and illusions, God's Will can be heard and followed, bringing an end to pain and hate.

Our Connection with Reality

To answer the illusory mistake of separation, we are given a connection with the Divine, who understands our illusions and can lead us safely through them. Since this guide is Love, it maintains for us the connection with Love that we would throw away. Being Love, it can only lead us as we are willing to be led. There is never any demand. The only pressure we feel comes from the self-imposed pain of not following the principles of harmony. This self-inflicted pain can be reduced to the extent that we are willing to reduce our desire to follow our individual will where it is opposed to Love's will. We may feel we are being asked to give up what we most love. This is an illusion. We are only giving up illusory love to find real love, illusory peace to find real peace, and illusory joy to find true joy. The illusory self we have created is the part of us that desires illusory things. This is not our real *being*. Since we are most familiar with the illusory experience, and our chosen identity is an illusory being, there can be a very real sense of loss as we give up our illusory creations. My personal experience is that in time I see there was no loss, but rather a new freedom and a greater gift awaiting me. I believe it is helpful to adopt an attitude of enjoyment of our present gifts, but a willingness for them to change at any time.

Following God's Will

So how do we seek God's Will? First, of course, by *listening*. That is accomplished by suspending our judgment, desires, and viewpoints. If a quiet mind is difficult to achieve because our personal investment in our perceived self makes it impossible to hear God's Voice, we can simply *accept* the situation and let Truth be revealed to us. In time, the real purpose always comes forth. Within every situation, even illusory ones, there are the seeds of God's Love. By simply desiring truth, love, peace, and joy for all concerned, we have done all we need to do. Even if we do not see the results immediately, they will come.

It has now been 20 years since my second divorce. For the first five years, I experienced a deep sense of grief. For the last 15 years I have seen, only partially at times, how it was the best thing for both of us. The one person I could not include in this loving perspective was the man whom I felt caused the divorce and who eventually became her husband. I could see nothing good about him, and it seemed impossible for me to be grateful for him. I now know that my judgment was very wrong. Recently he passed away. As I talked with my ex-wife about her experiences since our divorce, I saw for the first time that their marriage was very important on a spiritual level. They both needed to share that experience together even if it was difficult at times. I saw that the outcome of their marriage was learning how to give each other unconditional love.

It has taken 20 years, but I now have my peace with the situation, even though it did not work out as I had originally hoped. I feel deep appreciation for my ex-wife's husband, who gave her spiritual gifts I could never give. I also know that she was very important in his spiritual growth. They were both very instrumental in my own spiritual life, too, for that divorce marked the beginning of my search for inner peace.

We do not have to know in advance what God's Will is. I doubt we ever will as long as we are human. We simply know that God's Loving principles always operate, and sometimes we are given the vision to see them in operation. If we seek Love for all concerned in each situation, and if that is what we truly desire, we will find ourselves easily aligned with God's Will. If we desire Truth to be revealed to all concerned, we will eventually find it. Following God's Will is not dependent upon our ability to fathom the Divine Mind or even our capacity to understand Divine Principles. If it was, few of us would ever be able to awaken. Following God's Will is simply trusting what is happening, and asking for clarity.

We need not try to put these Truths into action; they are already in action. We simply need to desire to see them clearly. Following God's Will, we desire to see Divine Truth, Love, and Joy in place of our individual illusory truth, love, and joy. The Real Will has, always and already, replaced the illusory will. We do not have to accomplish anything; we can just quietly wait. This attitude aligns us easily. As we wait quietly for clarity, it will be revealed. We need never worry about that; it will be shown to us and done through us.

The Power of Being

Being is the opposite of *power* in this world. Its effects are not the result of great strength or prodigious effort. *Being's* energy flows naturally and feels as if every force is directed toward the same end. It is not a superior force overcoming a resistant force. It is a feeling of the absence of any resistant force. In fact, at the level of *being,* one feels that no resistance is possible. It is a rhythm, a dance, and a merging of forces into no force.

Living in this space, even for a short time, feels very natural. Grace seems to move in front of us, overcoming and harmonizing all discord before it reaches us. We may see the discord approaching, but it will never affect us—that is the amazing thing. *Being* is effortless and simple, and while we are in this harmony, we wonder why life ever seemed to be any other way. While this harmony cannot be achieved by effort, it can be experienced. This is our natural state, and our fears and doubts create the unnatural state where we believe power and strength are necessary. The fear that creates the unnatural state of conflict also maintains it.

As we apply more power and effort to avoid opposition, we thereby create an opposing force that resists us.

Much like stretching a rubber band to its limit, as one proceeds to stretch it, more effort is needed to maintain the stretched rubber band. The end result is that the rubber band snaps back if increased strength is not applied. The rubber band is not resisting your efforts; it is just trying to return to its natural state. That is very similar to what happens in our life. We apply greater and greater effort to difficult situations until they reach the breaking point or we do. We also have the choice of letting them remain in a natural state, which requires no effort.

The Three Steps of Being

These three steps of awareness might be called "doubter," "observer," and "blesser." I separate things into phases and steps in my books as a method of explanation. Maybe this is a good place to say that all this is merely an attempt to make these processes understandable and to give memorable guidelines along the way. There are no steps or separate processes of *listening, accepting*, and *being*. They are all one. It is also not quite true that they are even steps. Looking back, I see that I was getting parts of the *being* phase all along and that *accepting* was part of *listening*, although I was never given that name at the time. So don't get too hung up on processes. Don't put too much emphasis on the completion of these steps. All measurement is just a human way of thinking. Having said that, let's look at these three steps, or better yet, these three awarenesses.

First—A Change of Perception

At first, I was aware while *listening* for guidance that I often did not see what was really happening. At times, I would be confused about what to do, but more often it was because I did not see the situation clearly. I remember once driving into Milan and realizing that the banks had closed and I needed a place to exchange francs. Everything downtown was closed, and I was unsure of what to do next. Then I looked up and saw a picture of an airplane just below a street sign. I then knew I needed to go to the airport, not a bank, because it would be open and I thought it would have a money exchange. At the airport, the exchange counter was closed, but a car rental place exchanged my money. I found them simply by asking a porter where to change money. Sometimes when I needed money changed, I might get distracted and later realize that I did not need to change currency after all. I never knew what would happen, and I was often shown that my perceived needs were not necessary. What I really wanted was a nice campsite, and that turned out to be located near the airport where I was directed by the car rental attendant.

My guidance these days is usually not in terms of how to do something, but rather a change in my perception. As this continues to happen, I become less concerned with my perceptions of my needs and more open to re-examining what is happening.

To me, this is the first step in *being,* the awareness that my perception of what is happening is always question-able. This is very much like the beginning step in the *listening* process, which I call *be still.* We open to our inner guide by the temporary suspension of our own thinking and the quieting of our mind. The state that occurs is one of withdrawal or distancing from a specific need or event. Before this awareness, we are convinced that we know what is happening and we know how to fix it. You may like to think of it this way: We take one step back from action and become less personally involved. We become a "doubter"—not knowing that we have the right solution to the situation. We open to other possibilities, even to the possibility that we may not have a problem.

Second—Letting Go of Personal Involvement

The second step keeps going in the same direction, away from concern about the situation and personal involvement. As I deepened my use of *accepting,* I realized that I did not know what was happening most of the time. Not that I did not have judgments, but I began to realize that my perceptions were quite narrow. I saw that I usually only looked at situations from a single point of view, my own. I tended to project that point of view on the entire situation and everyone involved. As I stopped wanting other people to act in a certain way, I could release them from my plans and desires. I could see that they viewed the situation from a very different standpoint. Now I am, if you like to think of it this way, two steps back from the situation. I can now see another's viewpoints and even question my own viewpoint. Even more spectacular is the beginning of the awareness that these other viewpoints may not be in conflict with mine, even though at first glance they may seem to be. I am now an "observer" of the situation and not a participant in it. This step brings clarity naturally by removing my desires and needs, as I perceive them, from the situation. It is not giving up these desires, but just stepping back from them so I can see more clearly.

Third—Join in the Oneness

There is at least one more step that removes me entirely from any situation and experience. Now that I can go farther away from the situation, I can give up any desire for it to be different. I can truly see that the situation, as it is, is best for all concerned. Only from a human standpoint of limited perceptions, such as limited life span, limited love, and limited truth can I see something wrong. While the situation may appear to be personally difficult, I can see that given the welfare of all those involved and everyone's need for increased spiritual awareness, what is happening is the best thing that can happen. I am now at least three steps removed from what I think I see.

This third step has been most difficult. When I first

wrote this section, I was in the final stages of selling the Retreat Center for the third time. Each time it had sold for less money, and it seemed that this last time I was giving it away. I had no security for my future and had lost a great deal of my investment. It seemed that the situation was not only very unfair, but personally it felt as if my good intentions and my willingness to trust others had backfired in my face. One of my major awarenesses from my seven years at the retreat was giving up the idea that I could be unjustly treated. Releasing the idea that as a good person I am entitled to some reward for my helping, caring, or trusting has been a major struggle in my life. I cannot look to others to appreciate me; I can only to look to the Divine to care for me in ways I cannot control. When I do "good" acts to get appreciation and rewards in return, I am still trying to control others and the outcome. Incidentally, my fears of not having any money never materialized, but I still don't know how it all works.

From a noninvolved point of view, this third step, I no longer see myself as harmed in any way. Even though I may not see all the blessings that will come to me, I know in my heart that all is well. As a blesser, I can be at peace, and I can love each person involved. While I may feel sadness that we have to go through difficult experiences, I know that what is happening is the most loving thing for all involved. While a situation is beyond my limited ability to understand, I can see enough to participate and bless all involved. Now I am naturally in the *being* state. I am at peace, and I see little to do when I choose to bless and release. That is all that needs to be done.

Our Being *Revealed*

Do not assume that you understand your *being*, for you will be wrong. You and I have a concept of our selves as humans. We learned this concept from our worldly consciousness. We try to be what the world says we should be. Even in our spiritual search, we adopt worldly ideas and worldly concepts of what is spiritual. These are human concepts of spiritual *being*. We then set out to reach this higher state, thinking that by so doing we will become spiritual. (For example, the term *higher state* is a human concept and not relevant spiritually, for there is no higher or lower in Reality.) Usually these concepts are simply ideas of what a good human being would be like. These worldly spiritual concepts miss the mark and entwine us in a web of frustration and self-denial. If we have to use great willpower to force ourselves to do what we have been told is spiritual and deny what we truly feel within ourselves, we can be sure we are on the wrong path. This should alert us that we are not following a natural, unfolding spiritual path.

In conclusion, I want to bless you for your interest in our spiritual awakening. As you can see, my own awakening is not a pretty thing. I cry, laugh, hate, love, curse, and bless. While much of the process is painful and difficult, the moments of revelation are awe-inspiring. More and more, I am able to see the humor in situations sooner and laugh in amusement rather than rail in anger. I am convinced, however, that it doesn't matter how I do it. It may even be that a path of struggle is my only path. If it is, my Jewish friends have told me I am not alone. I have not verified what they've told me, but I love the idea. They say that the word *Israel* means "those who wrestle with God." I guess I am right at home with a nation of God wrestlers. If you want to know more about wrestling with God, reread the Jacob story in the Old Testament. I especially love the end, where the angel who has wrestled with Jacob all night begs in the morning to be let go. Jacob, who pretty much lost the fight, says, "I won't quit until you bless me." Now his name is changed to Israel, and he is told he will be the father of many nations.

Our *Being* is the end of this struggle. We do not need to fight to bring about change, for no change is necessary. We do need to hold on during the struggle until we get the blessing.

Thank you again for joining with me. We will meet again, maybe with the publication of my next book.

God Blesses You.

Being Statement

God is my being
From my being I know
What I need is provided
What I do is successful
What I think is peaceful
What I see is true
What I feel is love
Because I am one

Ten Principles of *Being*

1. I accept my Self as I am in Reality.

2. I release all need to control.

3. I release all concepts about myself and others.

4. I desire only inner peace.

5. I live only in this moment.

6. I allow my essence, my real *"being,"* to manifest.

7. I desire joy in all my experiences.

8. I join my will with God's Will.

9. I always ask, "What do I really want?"

10. I give to others all that I give myself.

*We are truly
One.*

About the Author

Nearly 20 years ago, Lee Coit began a quest for answers to his pain and frustration. He decided to devote an entire year to this search, and as a result, he discovered an inner guidance system. Since that time he has followed this inner voice in making the important decisions in his life. This path has led to a peaceful and happy life, the writing of several books that have international distribution, and to giving lectures and workshops throughout the United States and Europe. For nearly ten years, he ran the Las Brisas Retreat Center. His dramatic change from a very busy advertising agency executive to a content and happy spiritual being gives hope to anyone who is seeking a better way to live.

Lee is available for lectures and seminars anywhere in the world and makes every effort to respond to all requests.

If you would like to attend a workshop, please send your name. If you want to sponsor such an event, please let us know, as sponsorship is quite easy. When we have enough interest for several workshops in one part of the world, we plan a trip to that area. Of course, we will offer lectures and workshops for almost any size group. The workshop can be held in a home or a public facility. We are primarily interested in the desire of the attendees to increase their spiritual awareness; we are not concerned with numbers, revenues, or exposure.

We offer either one- or two-day sessions, and also longer workshops if there is a desire. If we are requested to make a special trip to an area, we ask that our travel expenses be covered in addition to the workshop fees. Please write for our complete brochure regarding sponsorship of an event if you are interested. We would be happy to discuss the matter with you. We would love to come to your area sometime and share this wonderful process with you and your friends.

For more information, please write to:

Lee Coit
1212 Ave. Buena Suerte
San Clemente, CA 92672

or e-mail:
brisas@ix.netcom.com

NOTES

We hope you enjoyed
this Hay House book.
If you would like to receive a free catalog featuring
additional Hay House books and products, or
if you would like information about the
Hay Foundation, please write or call:

Hay House, Inc.
P.O. Box 5100
Carlsbad, CA 92018-5100
(800) 654-5126 • (800) 650-5115 (fax)

Please visit the Hay House Website at:
http://www.hayhouse.com